Buildings
Are for People

Buildings
Are for People

Human
Ecological
Design

BILL CAPLAN

First published in 2016 by Green Frigate Books

Green Frigate is an imprint of Libri Publishing

Copyright © Libri Publishing Ltd.

ISBN: 978-0-9933706-1-8

A CIP catalogue record for this book is available from The British Library

Book and cover design by Carnegie Book Production

Printed by Hobbs the Printer Ltd.

Libri Publishing
Brunel House
Volunteer Way
Faringdon
Oxfordshire
SN7 7YR

Tel: +44 (0)845 873 3837

www.libripublishing.co.uk

Dedicated to all those
who strive to make the built environment
a better place for people.

Contents

Championing the Social–Ecological Context of Architecture

In *Buildings are for People – Human Ecological Design*, Bill Caplan issues a clarion call for the design/build professions to expand their concept of sustainable design to be more inclusive of the social, as well as the physical, environment. Doing so, Caplan delivers what might be regarded by some as being nothing less than a manifesto urging architects to do a better job of interlinking people with ecosystems, at what he calls the "human ecological interface". Buildings, we are reminded, are much more than physical edifices that are *constructed*; rather, they can transform and in some cases actually *create* the ambient surroundings that they occupy. As Charles Dickens instructs in *Pickwick Papers*, there is an important lesson for architects in the distinction to be made between the two words that I have italicised in the preceding sentence, for "the whole difference between construction and creation is exactly this: that a thing constructed can only be loved after it is constructed; but a thing created is loved before it exists."[1]

Buildings are for People is, as its title states, above all else about our relationships to the built environments we create and inhabit. According to Caplan, "the fundamental value of architecture resides in its service to humanity"; and "the language of architecture is experiential – it is interactive". In this latter regard, those of us blessed with an appreciation of beauty and recognition of sense of place hold deep admiration for our favourite buildings. In a peripatetic fashion, Caplan delivers his thesis with frequent reference to some of his own favourite buildings, carefully chosen to illustrate the technical points in the text. "Architecture", he states, "is the *interface* of human ecology, a buffer among people, and a buffer between people and the natural world." Today, many years on, I still fondly remember my first glimpse of Pharaoh Hatshepsut's mortuary temple – its colonnaded and stepped platforms a brilliant geo-mimicry of the cliffs and perched ledges rising above; as well as the physics-mimicry of the Fibonacci series spiralling in the roof of one of the buildings at the wonderful Eden Project in Cornwall. Such engendered feelings lie at the heart of what we carry away from interacting with the sort of memorable buildings that Caplan refers to as exhibiting the quality of "environmental harmony".

What becomes obvious in reading this book is that the profession of architecture has much to improve upon if it is to deliver the goods and services required to be part of the holistic paradigm advanced in these pages. In this regard, *Buildings are for People* joins the growing chorus of criticisms that have been raised about the motivations and methodologies in the design/build world.[2] For herein, Caplan provides an honest consideration of the obstacles that must be circumvented, including, for example, a crippling obsession with aesthetic design and vapid symbolism; the placeless intrusion of inappropriate and even "harmful" structures out of all context with their surroundings; the triumph of image over essence that gives rise to greenwash; and an educational system that is sorely in need of reform.

On the flip side, and more importantly, Caplan offers constructive insight into how things can be improved, such as his emphasis on energy and experience as being the co-determinants for adjudicating any building's performance in the physical and social environments, respectively. In the end, *Buildings are for People – Human Ecological Design* is a guidebook for achieving positive change in the way we reconfigure our world and our place therein. As such, it should find prominent position on the shelf beside other like-minded and worthy tomes that challenge and encourage us all to do better.[3]

Robert L. France,
Dalhousie University

Notes

1   This distinction has been noted by environmental managers involved in wetland design and creation projects, for example: Salveson, D., *Wetlands: Mitigating and Regulating Development Impacts*, Urban Land Inst., 1994; and France, R.L., *Wetland Design: Principles and Practices for Landscape Architects and Land-use Planners*, W.W. Norton, 2003.

2   The corpus of this criticism is both voluminous and, at times, quite pointed, including, for example: Silber, J., *Architecture of the Absurd: How "Genius" Disfigured a Practical Art*, Quantuck Lane Press, 2007; Meades, J., "Architects are the last people who should shape our cities: New, shiny buildings are all well and good, but what architects forget is a sense of place – and the beauty of wastelands", *Guardian*, 12 Sept. 2012; as well as my own efforts in this regard: France, R.L., "Smokey mirrors and unreflected vampires: From eco-revelation to eco-relevance in landscape design", *Harvard Design Magazine* 10 (Spring/Summer 2000): 36–40; "Green world, gray heart? The promise and reality of landscape architecture in sustaining nature", *Harvard Design Magazine* 13 (Spring/Summer 2003): 30–36; and *Veniceland Atlantis: The Bleak Future of the World's Favourite City*, Libri Publishing, 2012.

3   Some of the favourites from my own library include: Lyle, J., *Design for Human Ecosystems: Landscape, Land Use, and Natural Resources*, Island Press, 1985; Thayer, R., *Gray World, Green Heart: Technology, Nature, and the Sustainable Landscape*, John Wiley and Sons, 1994; and Steiner, F., *Human Ecology: Following Nature's Lead*, Island Press, 2002.

Architecture Transforms Space

We transform the generality of *space* into the uniqueness of *place* through the act of building. This enterprise defines our built environment, creating new interfaces with people and the natural environment. *Buildings are for People – Human Ecological Design* addresses the design of those interfaces, seeking to benefit people and sustain our ecosystem.

Architecture activates the character, the physical attributes and the tenor of a space, generating a sense of place. Therein lies the magic of architecture. The interactions among *the buildings we erect, the natural environment* and *people* constitute the relationships of "human ecology"; all three possess the ability to enhance our quality of life and at the same time interact responsibly with nature. These are the goals of *human ecological design* – creating people-friendly and eco-friendly interventions. "Buildings", "people" and "environments" are its focus.

Buildings and their infrastructure constitute the built environment. We construct them for human benefit – to serve people. Symbioses with the natural environment are essential to their long-term success. Nevertheless, in real-estate development, the quest for profit often trumps the interests of the inhabitants, the community and our ecosystem. In institutional architecture, imagery often trumps program efficacy. This need not occur. Human interests, aesthetics and sustainability can be compatible with profit – by design.

Human ecological design engages the client's purpose, the human experience and the qualities of our natural environment. It addresses individuals and the community in their zones of interaction. While meeting client needs, it aims to achieve a beneficial intervention that nurtures the occupants, visitors, passersby and neighbourhood in a symbiotic relationship with nature. A work of architecture – driven by the client's agenda with its goals, program and budget – can transform a space into a place in surprising ways. It is a physical structure, an arrangement of natural or manmade materials, yet its outcome can arouse one's mental sensibilities, emotions and spirituality beyond its physical interactions with the community and the environment. The built environment, an integral part of human ecology, alters our living environment in material and experiential ways, shaping the character of *human experience*, the physical, mental and economic wellbeing of individuals and the community at large.

However, satisfying a client's agenda alone does not ensure a positive outcome; an intervention can catalyse both beneficial and detrimental interactions. Globally, one can encounter urban and suburban buildings that fail to integrate successfully with their surroundings, or to establish propitious relationships with their larger environments. This often occurs as an unintended result of limited or faulty design. Buildings whose architecture captures public enthusiasm from an aerial perspective often lack such qualities at street level where daily life interfaces with the built environment. Many cities evidence this failure of comprehensive design – New York, Houston, Beijing and Dubai, for example – and many suburbs as well. Architects can do better.

Buildings are for People – Human Ecological Design speaks to all those concerned with the state of building around the world and its impact on people, their communities and the ecosystem upon which we depend. It is dedicated to architects, planners, engineers, developers and policy makers – the students, educators and practitioners who will envision, enable and create tomorrow's built environment. I seek to encourage architectural design that is sensitive to the interrelationships of human ecology as the norm.

A commentary on architecture's purpose and the value of "green" design, this book offers a new approach to *the process of conceiving* architectural design, a methodology inspired by the formative elements of human ecology – people, the natural environment and the built environment. The methodology posits architecture as a physical, sensible and operative interface that *separates* and *creates* environments, *meshing* their characteristics. It recognises that once built, works of architecture alter the very environment they occupy. It conceptualises the building envelope through the lenses of architecture, human ecology and engineering, with some help from neuroscience. Through these perspectives, the notion of *interdependency* illuminates a new approach to design, a new way of thinking – architecture as a *human ecological interface*. With the aid of photographs and illustrations, this exploration probes the ways in which we perceive the energy inherent in architecture's shape and form, and how architecture interacts with the energy of our ecosystem – all of which intertwine.

The **Introduction** explores the meaning of architecture and its significance, the concept of human ecological design, and the ever-present interplay of energy. In the subsequent chapters, serial concepts unroll a rational approach seeking to develop an *ecological foundation* for the *process of conceiving design*, while also considering many of the obstacles. A new methodology for modelling the building envelope unfolds. The model emerges from a building's physical and experiential interfaces, their interactions with people, with nature's elements and with the pre-existing built environment.

The thesis develops in three sections: 'Buildings Intervene', 'The Struggle for Green' and 'Human Ecological Design'. It explores the influences of architecture, local context and the environment on each other and on human perception, with an eye toward *multifunctional* synergies. Striving to foster *inter*dependent thinking, its principles endeavour to catalyse site-based designs, sensitive to the interplay of human instinct, perception and response in synergy with our natural environment. The process addresses the interdependency of *architecture and people* with *energy and our ecosystem*, in the context of architectural practice.

My purpose is to encourage the establishment of a meaningful *place* through architecture, an architecture responsive to the fundamental aspects of human experience, which provides a positive experiential interrelationship between people and the built environment in a sustainable manner that functions harmoniously with our ecosystem.

Bill Caplan

Human Ecology
People – The Built Environment –
The Natural Environment

"Buildings are built for people" is an obvious truism. Yet much of our building over the last half-century belies that truism in all but its simplest interpretation, especially in urban and suburban areas. Profit, expediency and prestige frequently trump human welfare, community and the natural environment.

The application of "sustainable design" to architecture often succumbs to a similar fate. A victim of profit, expediency or "green-wash" marketing, it frequently fails to achieve sustainable benefit during its cradle-to-grave life cycle.

We are increasingly aware of the interplay between our built environment and nature's ecosystem, its potential to foster a productive and healthful ecology or to do us harm. We, the people, are part of that interplay, the *interdependent relationships* that comprise *the essence of human ecology*. These relationships are animated by *the exchange of energy*, and the *interactions* of people, the built world and our planet's natural environment. The energy of these interactions manifests in numerous forms significant to the effectiveness of architecture.

The more cognisant we are of these interactions, and the more we draw on their qualities during the architectural design process, the more *human* and *ecological* our built environment will become. Our growing understanding of human perception, interaction and healthful living highlights the relationships between architecture and human response, while ongoing research continues to shed new light on humanity's impact on the ecosystem. In tandem with enhanced analytics, this expanding knowledge base enables us to confront the built environment's ecological influence *proactively*.

New technologies, toolsets and materials, and an ecological inclination, mean that we are well-positioned to design buildings that engage current and future lifestyles with environmental harmony. We have the ability to integrate technological advances with an insightful design process, fostering designs that are responsive to both people and the natural environment while meeting the needs of the client. This is the essence of *human ecological design*: designing a client's architecture in harmony with people and the natural environment. *Human ecological design is proactive.*

The Applications Gap

Even in this new millennium, despite new insights concerning human ecology and the availability of new design methods, architectural practice continues to rely on outdated values and old DNA. Given the waning interest in revivalist transformation and classical reference used more for historical perspective than as a touchstone for comparison, this seems especially odd.

Architecture schools offer abundant exploratory opportunity, much of it enabled by the expanding accessibility of computer power and user-friendly software. Increased memory and processor speed at decreased cost have broadened access to a proliferation of design and sustainability oriented programs. Computers and the Internet also facilitate collaboration, communication and processing, as well as instant access to current innovation and digital graphic content. However, although architectural curricula teach the concepts of contextual design and the principals of sustainability in concert with computer modelling, increasing course requirements leave little time to tackle the gap between creative concept and fruitful application. The same is true concerning the availability of new materials and building technologies.

In professional practice, working with tight client budgets or timeframes, many architectural firms lack the resources to utilise innovative techniques. Formidable innovations available to architects such as computer-simulated design, new materials and building techniques, and the science of sustainable design have so far realised minimal benefit to society or the built environment. As this knowledge base rapidly expands, little fruitful benefit makes its way to the profession. The consequences reinforce the use of outdated designs, unintended *misuse* of new ideas and technology, and the continuation of uninspired building practices to maximise profit.

Resistance within the design/build professions to adopt emerging design philosophies, techniques and their toolsets remains greater than ever. Minimal opportunity exists for the implementation of state-of-the-art design methodologies without prostituting ingenuity in favour of expediency, disingenuous substitution or profit. Commentaries, critiques, seminars and design reviews worldwide evince dissatisfaction with the state of new building.

Sustainable design features intended to reduce the consumption of non-renewable resources, by using renewable sources and decreasing waste, frequently miss their goals. Calculations of their purported benefits often ignore material and equipment life cycles, and the energy expended mining raw materials and in manufacture, transportation, installation and disposal or reprocessing. Minimising environmental impact while lowering energy cost is attainable, but it requires realistic assessments. *There is a gap to overcome between our design capabilities and their application.*

We can enhance the built environment more productively. A society with such vast resources, depth of knowledge, and understanding of the hurdles can extract true benefit from its science, engineering and design capability. From an engineering perspective, the possibilities for advancing architectural effectiveness seem limitless. Computer simulations of parametric influences, that incorporate design and technological solutions for ecologically responsive architecture, provide the means. Conceptualising the building envelope as both a human and an environmental interface enhances that capability. With a meaningful methodology to alter the design vocabulary, parametric scrutiny of human ecological interrelationships enables more than a conceptual fantasy. A human ecological mindset that stimulates creative thinking can fertilise success.

Fortunately, there exist visionary architects who truly incorporate new thinking with architectural design. Nonetheless, the overall profession needs assistance to avoid reinventing the old, reincarnating style rather than innovative conception – overlooking *how* people and the environment interface with architecture.

Architecture: Theoretical Argument, Art or Function?

To the question "how do you define architecture?" my history/theory professor replied: "I am not going there!"[1] With a short historical review, it took little time to appreciate that response. To many, the word "architecture" refers to the design of a building or structure, embracing its conception, scheme, style and the realisation of a built entity. The result occupies a physical space that is separate from, yet part of, a larger ecosystem. With its own identity and systematic structure, this entity materialises as a place within a place, a particular environment within an environment.

The criteria that classify a building as a work of *architecture* are often a function of one's perspective – architect, academic, critic or developer, client or the public. The criteria carry wildly varying subjective connotations. Their standards vary in scope from a composition's theoretical underpinnings, to style or some mark of distinction. However, in common terms, "architecture" constitutes both an art and a science; attending to the program, plan, design and erection of buildings. Often synonymous with a building's style, the term "architecture" sometimes refers to the building itself.

Historically, the mere act of building does not necessarily produce what is termed *architecture*. This is evident in Vitruvius' first-century BC "Fundamental Principles of Architecture"[2], in twenty-first-century writings, and during the intervening two thousand years. Periodically, throughout history, themes of universal beauty and the elevation of human creativity surface concerning the cultivation and enlightenment of architecture, music, art, literature, poetry and science. Addressing architecture, these aspirations often encourage the pursuit of an ideal over a functional outcome; the achievement of high purpose over primary needs; and refinement, theory or novelty over effectuation.

A common allegory in architectural writings explains the origin of manmade shelters, whereby primitive humanity sought shelter beyond indigenous caves and dugouts. In this allegory, primitive humans assemble a simple structure – the *primitive hut* – having been inspired by observations of nature, encountered by happenstance. Vitruvius introduced this contrivance in "The Origin of the Dwelling House" in *De archituria libri decem (De architectura)*[3], believed to be the first treatise devoted solely to architecture. Rediscovered in 1414[4] and printed in 1486, this work has served as a reference for architects ever since. The allegory proffers a logical fable as to why and how manmade structures emerged. But were they *architecture*? Given that they were built by instinct or superficial imitation, do they qualify? Vitruvius posits to the origins of the art of building, yet provides little insight into the origins of architecture.

For some, the classical Greek construction documented by Vitruvius symbolises the genesis of *architecture*: rooted by a dependency on concepts of form, structure, appropriateness and beauty – more than happenstance, an expression of theory. His "Fundamental Principles of Architecture" define architecture to be dependent on "Order, Arrangement, Eurythmy[*], Symmetry, Propriety and Economy"[5] – executed by an architect. Architectural education includes history, philosophy, music, medicine, astronomy and theory of the heavens, among other things[6] – an impressive list. To Vitruvius, architecture was the product of art and theory. He set the stage for debate.

The premise that architecture depends upon theory remains today, whether derived from a new concept, materials or technology, or otherwise. In his 2011 work *The Autopoiesis of Architecture*, Patrik Schumacher proposed a redefinition of the fundamental principles of architecture with a new "contemporary style"[7] facilitated by computer aided design relationships based on sophisticated computer algorithms that shape form. His thesis maintains the restrictive view that architecture *depends upon theory*, not on the outcome.

> Architectural theory is integral to architecture in general and to all architectural styles in particular: there is no architecture without theory… Architecture in contrast to mere building is marked by radical innovation and theoretical argument.[8]

---

[*] Eurythmy signifies the proportion and rhythm of a harmonious structure.

Yet the debate over architecture's validity or substance is often associated with historical periods such as Roman, Ottoman, Byzantine or Gothic. For Schumacher "architecture proper only begins with the Renaissance."[9] Frank Lloyd Wright espoused the antithetical view of the Renaissance: "It is the setting sun which we mistake for dawn."[10]

The notion that architecture *must* arise from theory as premeditation and postulation, as a cognitive innovation grounded in societal hierarchy and mores, continues to obfuscate a meaningful definition. In some circles, the term "architecture" implies the attainment of a certain character, quality and intent. Champions of this characterisation promote their own standards and aesthetics. Designating exaltation or stature as touchstones minimises the fundamental value of architecture. As most buildings lack specific ideologies, theoretical constructs, emotive content or a significant means of distinction, such beliefs prompt the conclusion that little of our built environment may be rightfully termed "architecture".

The term "architecture" need not persist as a value system arbitrated only by a coterie of theorists and professional critics, a value system that authenticates the genetic makeup of architecture, its DNA. Perhaps we should scale the criteria relative to the means and values of its era and circumstances: the knowledge, cognitive development, aesthetics and toolset of its own time, culture and locale. After all, relative to its time and circumstances, a *primitive hut* is no less purposeful than an acknowledged work of architecture, and it may even demonstrate order, arrangement, eurythmy, symmetry, propriety and economy, or a pragmatic construct.

Built architecture does not require theoretical discourse to justify a building's existence; worth resides in the efficacy of the building's interface with *people*, their *program* and the *environment*. The use of dogmatic criteria to judge a building's merit fails to capture its principal significance, *its role in human survival, development and enrichment.*

Architectural purpose originates from the program. Site constraints and a contextual theme drive a design, the initial plan from which structure and elevation concepts develop. Some say a design emerges. The program, plan or elevation might provide the primary inspiration, the determinant of form, or perhaps they will all work together in tandem. Two thousand years of architectural theory proffer a multitude of guiding principles ad infinitum: "form follows function", "interior determines exterior", "elevation emerges from plan", "form expresses structure", and the like. Ultimately, whatever the guiding principles (if any), a design gestates, form develops – a building materialises. Its value relates to human employment.

Success, while deeply entwined with metrics of the programmatic function, conjointly depends on its holistic value to the local community and environment. To achieve this, architecture must be beneficial to the user, the passerby and the environment, as well as to client and program.

Removed from the arbitrary values of theorists and critics, personal style prefer-ence, historical reference, pedigree or structural theory, *the interactive properties of built architecture reveal its true virtues* – the way it functions.

Architecture's facility to mediate environments and places, as both a physical and sensible intermediary, is its most powerful attribute. When conceived through this interfacial paradigm, architecture affords many opportunities to enhance our lives as well as our surroundings regardless of scale – from a primitive hut to a grand cathedral to a palace of sport. Architecture is the *interface* of human ecology, a buffer among people, and a buffer between people and the natural world.

Architecture is Function

We may conceive architecture as a *rule of order that defines a transition* from one system to another, one environment to another, manifest as their common boundary. Whether real or imaginary, this *interface* is more than a mere surface that separates. Architecture is an interfacial system with substance and interactive surfaces. The surfaces transmit, communicate or catalyse, they input and output – to and from – one order to another, one environment to another. Analogous to a "black box", the interfacial substance regulates a transition – morphing the inputs to outputs through the black box's function. Whether embodied as a physical or a computational structure, architecture is a *system* that orchestrates *transformation*. The interface itself *is* the architecture.

Architecture in the *built* environment consists of manmade interfaces that distin-guish places, one from another: exterior from interior, interior from interior or from multiple exteriors. They generate interior places amidst an external environment, systems that embody a transforming function. Architectural interfaces mediate environmental transition by means of their material section. Spatial plan and circulation articulate the exterior and interior program.

The concepts in this book apply to architecture understood in the context of an interface, one that negotiates with *all* the environments in which a building arises and that the architecture itself creates. Emphasis on the "all" prevails. The ideas explored here seek to shed new light on the way we regard the architectural envelope, especially its process of conception.

Human ecological architecture derives from the interaction of energy and matter in the pursuit of function. *Energy,* its existence and expression, a unifying thread in the human ecological vocabulary, provides sustenance for our survival, emotional state, wellbeing and aesthetic satisfaction, as well as the means for both human perception and action.

With multiple embodiments, the multitudinous *manifestations of energy* are not always apparent. Our response to *shape, form, materiality* and *texture,* and their expressions of energy, reveal *interactions among people, architecture and energy.* The qualities of shape and form, materiality and texture embody energy, they actualise the interchange of energy and physical expression, transforming or restating its essence. They interact with light, heat, sound and other forms of energy informing and influencing human perception, cognition, emotion and action. They constitute the substance and language of architecture. How we perceive those interactions – how we *see, sense and interpret reality* – is integral to how we relate to architecture.

Ecologically designed interfaces promote the beneficial intersection of human experience and the energy vectors of nature, things manmade and the community. They negotiate these junctures of energy in its many forms. Aside from obvious sources such as the sun, earth temperature, weather and gravity, energy is also inherent in sound, electric and magnetic fields, chemical reactions and physical force. Energy is evident in light emitted or reflected from what we see, airflow, vibration, the movement of people and the life cycle of plants, trees and other living things. The built environment and nature shape these energy fields and vectors.

Energy is the animating force of human ecology; energy *interchange* is the essential mechanism of human ecological design.

Human Ecological Design: Designing for People in Harmony with our Existing Built and Natural Environments

The *physical interface of human ecology* is realised in the building envelope. One cannot design it by formula, by puzzling solutions to maximise yield, by indiscriminately erecting to the allowable building lines, or window dressing a conventional box. Human ecological architecture emerges from the interface of the program and its global surroundings in a holistic conception.

The holistic approach to architecture addresses its interaction with the components of human ecology as well as the program, budget and other constraints: community, society, the natural and the built environments. When addressed together, they provide the framework for a beneficial intervention. It can emerge on any lot, be sustainably efficient, adhere to zoning, meet code and provide an appropriate yield for the developer.

Human ecological architecture is inherently *contextual* – relational to its universe. It requires a design process that addresses the coincident influences of environment, people and program. These are reciprocal relationships, whereby each element of influence *influences* each of the others, the resultant design itself an influence. This admixture of interrelationships promulgates an interfacial exchange between people and their surroundings, enabling human ecological design on many levels.

As an *interfacial system*, architecture defines space and influences environmental character. The program defines the purpose and the budget – site, zoning and building codes dictate the constraints. A client's measure of success refers to the client's directives – the program, purpose, outreach, aesthetics, economics and, sometimes, environmentally conscious design. There is no universal mandate requiring a positive relationship with the community or the environment. Nor are beneficial aesthetics, environmental compatibility and societal value intrinsic properties of architecture. They are contextual qualities achieved through thoughtful design.

This book aims to elevate our awareness of the unavoidable interplay of people, the things people create and the natural environment, our awareness of their mutual impact on each other. *Consciousness* is the first step toward achieving a more human friendly and eco-healthy built environment.

We no longer build the "primitive hut" for our shelter. We have journeyed from *adapting to* the environment for survival to *creating* our environment, and in so doing we *alter* our ecosystem. Understanding how we physically interact with the environment and how our built environment interfaces with our lives has become more important. These ecological interactions are of our making.

The methodology promulgates a new framework of thinking to seed the creative process, one that reflects human instinct, the manner in which we perceive things, and environmental reality. Neither a design manual nor a set of rules, this book does not offer suggested floor plans, elevations or master plans, nor does it require or inhibit novel thinking or dictate style. Its objective is to promote a *consciousness* from which to germinate design; one that is applicable to all styles and all budgets based on human ecological principles. *Creative conception remains with the architect.*

It is Time to Reconsider the Obvious

Architects understand the need to respect our environment, to address context and to stimulate human perception. Unfortunately, the realities of building, budgets and time often get in the way. In the building industry, as in other industries, profit motivates and projects are born from opportunity. Human purpose often gets lost in that pursuit.

Although social themes, waste and pollution, sustainability, energy generation, sensory value and the like are frequent subjects for architectural competitions, art installations and educational displays, the portrayals are generally symbolic – fantasy. We need to address our built environment in its reality.

The building design and construction industry is a competitive, client-driven world. Whether a project results from institutional expansion or real-estate development, a combination of funding, profit and timeframe tend to drive the momentum – favouring prestigious design at one end and low-cost solutions at the other. When the agenda includes energy or sustainability ratings, qualifying for points often outweighs substantive value. In actual practice, beyond the aesthetic goals, an architect's mindset is specification driven. "What could be" takes a back seat, but this need not be so.

It is time to step back and reflect on the meaning of context – the design synergies it offers. It is time to reflect on the purpose of sustainability – how to net meaningful gain. It is time to examine our twenty-first-century goals and reset our mindset of what we can accomplish by design. We possess the tools, technologies, methodologies and materials to design more productive buildings within the confines of a client's program. To do so, we need to *rethink the obvious*, taking advantage of architectural creativity and engineering ingenuity.

All architecture touches people – everyone: occupants, visitors, passersby and the community. All architecture impacts the natural environment. Nonetheless, a building's primary purpose is to house a program. Style and aesthetics follow, but "green" living and community welfare are often afterthoughts.

The fundamental value of architecture resides in its service to humanity. When the creative process addresses the broad relationships of *human ecology*, and not only the needs of a client's program, we serve people more effectively.

We start by exploring how we interact with the built environment – its interfaces, interventions and the building envelope.

1   BUILDINGS INTERVENE

① *Interfaces Enable Change*

Architecture spawns interfaces
– common boundaries that define a rule of order.

▶ INTERFACIAL ARCHITECTURES –
Natural and Manmade Transformations

On a cold December morning while letters tapped on a tablet's glass interface composed a chapter of this book, snowflakes fell gently, blanketing white. Thoughtful taps on the tablet's lit letters were interrupted by occasional glances at snow-laden branches. From my sheltered room, perceptions of nature, people, buildings and energy came together through manmade *interfaces* – viewed though a glass window, expressed through a computer's interactive glass surface. Touching the "send" icon transformed words made visual by energy – ideas, feelings and metaphors – into text transported by energy, email processed by interfaces – all controlled by interfacial architectures.

The tablet computer is a manmade electro-mechanical interface, transforming touch and the body's electrical properties into optical and electrical parameters. Thoughts and sounds, through electrical and mechanical inputs, become visible and audible symbols transmitted as electrically coded data. Eye–brain and sensory system interfaces – human interfaces – mediate these symbols; evoking thought, emotion and physical response. The window too is a physical interface, separating interior from exterior yet transmitting light, view, sound and heat. Both of these glass interfaces were created by people, their performance regulated by their architecture.

Outside my window, water droplets crystallise, energy embodies in a frozen state. Delicate fractal patterns of lace form snowflakes, patterns exploding from the droplets. Fragile nothings knit together, floating to earth. Almost weightless, they accumulate in a blanket losing identity to the white mass – densely heavy or fluffy and light. Layers accumulate, gaining structure, pattern, texture and potential energy from fragile snowflakes to an aggregate mass, capable of chaotic disintegration or catastrophic energy release. Somewhere a snow bank emerges, feet-thick layers accumulate on a mountaintop. Layers blanket layers above a village – beauty, muffled sounds and serenity. Suddenly a small sound from silence, an artful snow-shift cleaves on a gleaming sunlit day, crackles and rumbles – an avalanche assumes mass and power. Order explodes in chaos, and chaos quiets to order – new architectures of energy and interfaces emerge. Then it melts, sublimates – disappears.

This natural progression results in a complex series of states and unstable *interfaces*: water|air, crystal|air, crystal|crystal, fluffy|dense, snow|ice, blanket|layer, layer|layer and layer|chaotic-fragmentation. Each physical state embodies interfacial characteristics, like a blanket of snow insulting a cabin roof or dormant spring plants. Even in a fleeting moment of a liquid transforming to a solid, or to a gas, an interfacial architecture exists – it is a rule of transformation between environments or systems. *Each interface possesses an architecture.* Each interface mediates an exchange of energy, molecules, particles or physical state. Their performance is determined by nature's architecture.

When a building materialises from an architect's ideas to an assemblage of components, *built interfaces* crystallise with materiality, structure, pattern, texture and physical qualities. They too embody energy in a complex series of states and interfaces. Each interface mediates exchanges of energy, molecules and particles, and sometimes a physical state. Each interface possesses an architecture created by human intervention. Each interface interacts with the architectures of nature and each interface interacts with people.

We interact physically and cognitively with our built and natural environments, through their physical interfaces, as well as our own *human interfaces*. Interfaces are more than a common boundary: they are an architecture of transition.

► ARCHITECTURE INTERVENES –
Affordance and Intrusion

The mere presence of built architecture constitutes an intervention in our ecological system. This physical materialisation, be it a building or infrastructure, intervenes with people's lives as well as the natural environment. It provides *affordances as well as intrusions.*

> "We make our buildings and afterwards they make us.
> They regulate the course of our lives."[11]
>
> Winston Churchill

Our built environment consists of manmade interfaces that bear directly on people and their communities and the elements of nature. Their interventions embody forces that intercede in our quality of life physically and mentally. They are intrusive, enabling and permeable at the same time, interacting with the community and nature, influencing both (Figure 1).

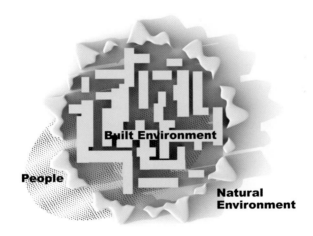

1. Human ecological relationships: the interfacing of people, the built environment and natural environment.

As an intervention, architecture is the sum of its *material, experiential* and *performative* manifestations, materialising the aesthetic and programmatic creations of the architect, and the operative functions of the engineer. Therein lies the power of design.

Each segment of the intervention is common to at least two environments, providing some combination of material, experiential and performative qualities; bridging those environments whether comprised of the structure's mass or its void, whether a barrier, portal or a permeable membrane. Each segment is an agent that regulates the transition of the environments it separates. In the hands of the architect and engineer, an architectural intervention can accomplish wondrous things.

Walls, roofs and floors enclose, divide and delineate space. They articulate architecture. More than just partitions or physical barriers, they facilitate *change* and *exchange*, managing the flow of energy from one space to another such as the passing of light, air, view and people. The components of built architecture are not passive objects: they are its active members – interactive within their physical assemblage, with people, with the program and with the immediate environment. Not only are they crucial to a building's physical function, but also to the exchange of energy and to human perception. A key to human ecological design, a building's components often merge, mingle and actively influence interactions in an indiscernible way.

Viewed through the *lens of architecture*, the components of architectural design are the means of materialising organisation, form and essence. The architect conceives a physical solution to a client's objective, the logic and spirit of its expression – the program environment, form and aesthetics. The architect develops a concept – expressed by the plan, structural philosophy, elevation, section, logistics and materiality. The product of this concept is the architecture, the creative response to a functional purpose, a physical interface that embodies the crystallisation of thought. The architectural interface emerges as an aesthetic form that invites and enables experiential interactions, a material form that intervenes in the built and natural environments.

Through the lens of architecture, interfaces emerge from the building envelope expressed by materials and form: arrangements of mass and void, texture and tone, space allocation and flow pattern. The form's characteristics define the occupant's environment. To the architectural designer, it includes the aesthetic and qualitative aspects of form, shape and volume.

Although building envelopes have existed since the earliest days of building enclosures, the term "building envelope" is loosely defined and means different things to architects, engineers, urban planners and developers. For example, in the context of local zoning regulations, the building envelope represents the three-dimensional building limit regulated by height, setbacks, use and other restrictions.

Through the *lens of engineering*, the building envelope is physically interactive. To meet the needs of the architect, the engineer's envelope comprises a coalition of mechanisms. Together they form a shell composed of barriers, filters, ports, supporting structures and operational systems. The barriers, filters and ports are mechanisms to accommodate porosity, passage, storage, deflection and obstruction. In its entirety, the engineer's envelope serves a physical function to withstand weather, to regulate air, acoustic quality and thermal exchanges, and to facilitate, catalyse and mediate changes in the state of the enclosed environments.

These material, experiential and performative perspectives bring to light a broad range of opportunities afforded by the properties of a building's surfaces and materiality, both the exterior and interior. Once recognised in this light, they become part of the designer's consciousness and toolset. Materialisation is the bailiwick of architects; mechanisms are the specialty of engineers.

Designing ecologically responsive architecture requires an additional lens, the holistic *lens of human ecology* with its broad perspective. The human ecological lens sheds light on numerous relationships among the program, its users and exterior influences, as well as contextual interactions with the community, the existing built environment and our ecosystem.

The lenses of architecture, engineering and human ecology challenge us to consider building design from multiple perspectives, enabling a designer to discover new potentials afforded by a human ecological point of view.

These interfaces that we build *catalyse interactions* – between our built environment and people, and our built environment and the natural environment. They are active and passive boundaries of materials and energy, intermediaries for both matter and the mind. Interfaces of the built environment take many forms that enable matter to interact or serve a function. Our built interfaces have the same ability to induce change as the interfaces of nature, creating order and wellbeing as well as chaos.

Built architecture's influence derives from its design; *design defines its influence.* Unlike snow, built entities do not disappear. Their substance enduringly interacts with the natural environment and enduringly affects the people in its sphere of influence.

▶ BUILDINGS ARE FOR PEOPLE – Human Shelter

Human shelter has evolved from creations of nature to creations of science – from earth and stone caves to curtain wall systems and high-technology structures. The architecture we build is replete with enabling opportunities to enrich and sustain life; energy is the animating force. Once built, it projects its influence with physical interaction and sensory stimulation; therein resides its ability to affect the world we live in. *New buildings impact all facets of human ecology* – people, the built environment and the natural environment.

We experience a building in both corporeal and sensory ways as it serves multiple spatial, programmatic and environmental functions. The arrangements of mass and voids form spaces and interconnections whose surfaces, substance and volumes create material, experiential and performative interventions. Architecture's elements are the means for its expression – the substance of its form and the mediators of its environments.

Created from an arrangement of substances, volumes and voids that fashion the tectonic and aesthetic, the building envelope comprises the *container of built design.* The notion of a *building envelope* seems straightforward: a structure's shell – skin and form. But there is more. In addition to its tangible presence, the building envelope physically and chemically interacts with the environment and elicits human experience. Parsing the envelope's tangible and sensible interplay with human ecology renders an expanded consciousness from which new design insight can emerge.

Intervening in the pre-existing, the built environment creates new spaces and places that enable living. *Architecture determines the qualities of interaction.* Not only does it influence a program's efficacy and the character of the local built environment, it bears directly on the natural environment and a community's wellbeing, altering them all in some fashion. The physical entity amends the aesthetic tissue; its mass, tectonic and emissions interact with nature and nature's inhabitants. Recasting the path of natural light and shadow, the emission and reflection of sound, and the circulation of air and rainwater as well as people, this intervention in human ecology is a stimulus for human experience; one that transforms the visual, audible, thermal and experiential order.

Appropriating, adapting and fabricating shelters, we have carved or assembled dwellings from an extraordinary variety of natural and manmade materials such as stone, ice, leaves, thatch, textiles, rice paper, concrete, metal, plastic, earth and glass. Figures 2 through 7 exemplify this broad range.

2. The Dark Church, carved in nature's envelope, sixth or seventh century, Cappadocia, Turkey. © Bill Caplan

3. Dung and branches. Maasai hut
in the Tanzania Serengeti.
© Bill Caplan

4. Sticks and reeds. Borana
hut in northern Kenya.
© Bill Caplan

5. Corrugated metal. Old Kibo Hut at
15,520ft (4,730m) on Mt. Kilimanjaro.
© Bill Caplan

7. Louvered metal facade.
Pan Nordic Embassies, Berlin,
Berger + Parkkinen Architekten.
© Bill Caplan

6. Bamboo, limestone, aluminium,
steel, glass. Madrid Barajas Airport,
Richard Rogers. © Bill Caplan

2 *Manifestations of the Building Envelope*

▶ PHYSICAL, SENSIBLE AND OPERATIVE – Embodied as One

The building envelope interacts with space, people and the environment in many ways. It defines and expresses the architecture.

All building envelopes have *physical*, *sensible* and *operative* characteristics that interface human ecology. All building envelopes have *surfaces* and *substance* that function as *barriers* and *ports*, empowered by means of their physical qualities and arrangement. By considering an envelope's interfaces from those perspectives, one can probe its potential for people-friendly *and* environment-friendly design.

Optimally, the elements of containment, expression and performance embody as one. Evaluating building materials and their potential for aesthetic expression, in conjunction with their physical properties and operating capabilities, enables architects to select those that enhance the performative qualities as well as the physical design. When aesthetic attributes work in harmony with their ecological universe, the users, the community and the client all benefit. In other words, overall benefit derives not only from how the envelope looks, but also from how the envelope works.

Materiality, Experience and Performance

Exploring a building envelope's relationships to the triad of human ecology – people, the pre-existing built environment and the natural environment – provides insight into many of the ecological efficacies that are available through creative architectural design. Each envelope context – its physical, sensible and operative manifestations – has a nuance that directly influences the way we live or the viability of our ecosystem.

A building envelope's 'physicality', the 'bricks and mortar' – its *materiality* – is an easily accessible context: it is the presence that occupies space and defines the building. In its 'sensible' context, the envelope *affords an experience*, enabling the visualisation, sensation and perception of shape, form, space, materiality and sense of place. In its 'operative' context, *the envelope is the means* for environmental and programmatic interactions, an interfacial system to weather the natural environment, control the flow of energy, manage the interior climate and enable the program.

Scrutinising surfaces, substances, barriers and ports in terms of their material, experiential and performative aspect enhances our awareness of architecture's multifaceted interface with human ecology. Embracing these distinctions generates a contextual approach to design inception, one that recognises these unique relationships in order to enable their holistic employment for aesthetic and performative potential – for how they look *and* how they work.

Each embodiment of the building envelope casts a sphere of influence on human ecology, one that can beneficially inform the design process. Each perspective provides a unique basis from which to scrutinise a design's potential, from its physical constitution, to our sensory impressions, to its corporeal and environmental interactions. Together, they describe its architectural presence within the community, its relationship to the existing built environment, its programmatic and environmental footprints, and the sense of place it creates.

They embody the tectonic and topographic qualities, programmatic qualities, emotive and sensory qualities and ecological qualities of architecture (Figure 8).

8. Physical, sensible and operative qualities of
the building envelope. Louisville Children's
Museum Competition entry, design and rendering
by author. © Bill Caplan

The building envelope is a three-dimensional *interactive system*: a physicality, toolset and experiential platform under the design control of architects and engineers, one that enables the orchestration of physical enclosure and energy interaction while creating a sense of place.

It is helpful to think of the building envelope in each of these modes as a *"material interface"*, an *"experiential interface"* and a *"performative interface"*. When a designer takes advantage of these interfacial opportunities to influence each component of the envelope, significant opportunities arise.

▶ MATERIAL INTERFACE –
The Physical Presence of Architecture

The arrangement, construction and qualities of matter that constitute a built entity structure a *physical* building envelope. The building envelope is a *material intervention*. Tangibly realised in the materiality of *skin* and *structure*, the physical envelope embodies a building's essence. It fixes boundaries and creates the spatial volume from which a program allocates the plan, materialising a scheme designed to meet the client's goal.

Having mass and dimensions, this embodiment not only represents but also objectifies the design concept, epitomising the composition's qualities, its order and classification. Weight bearing to enclose three-dimensional space, the physical envelope requires support from a skeletal system or an exoskeletal skin. When integral with the skin, support is a quality of the envelope.

The covering constitutes its skin, conforming to the envelope. Composed of multiple components, the skin articulates the architecture, *physically interfacing* with the exterior world *and* the enclosed space. Access, egress, portals and viewports enunciate the envelope's composition, as do the building's shell and foundation. The physical envelope is an *assembly of barriers and ports* (figures 9 and 10).

Surface skin such as a glass curtain wall, a structural skin such as concrete or an exterior system such as a rain shield or building-integrated solar panels may comprise portions of the physical envelope. So may portals and voids, even when embodied as an array of columns, perforations or artefacts.

Whether composed of skin, structure or both, the envelope's design is a *composition of materials*, whose character and arrangement suggest the building's physical nature. While many materials can portray an envelope's form, the qualities of these materials – not just their spatial arrangement – inform architecture's persona.

9. An envelope's barriers and ports.
House in Florianopolis, Brazil.
© Bill Caplan

10. An envelope's barriers and ports. TWA
Terminal 5, JFK Airport, Eero Saarinen, 1962.
© Bill Caplan

▶ EXPERIENTIAL INTERFACE –
The Sensible Presence of Architecture

The overall character of a building's envelope and one's street-level perception of the facade can be quite different – the difference between an architect's vision and the reality of its community interaction. When successfully executed, an envelope enunciates the designer's intention, expressing the architecture's overall character as well as its detail, intimating the visual qualities, style and aesthetic they embody. But does the street interface address passersby and the community as well? With thoughtful design, some do – but many more do not, even some with high-profile iconic designs. Positive community interface is not the norm, but it easily could be.

The Hancock Tower (1976), designed by Henry Cobb of I.M. Pei & Partners, is an excellent example of conscious design to address the community element of human ecological design. The introduction of a massive office tower directly across the street from H.H. Richardson's 1877 Trinity Church and Boston's historic Copley Square would have a major impact on the scale, aesthetic nature and human quality of the area. Cobb placed the community value of Trinity Church and the square on equal footing with the client's desire to build an iconic headquarters.

With a few clever design strokes, Cobb employed shape, surface and substance to defeat the impact of the building's enormous mass at sixty-two storeys above grade, two million square feet. Rather than set the building back into its site, high-lighting its mass from Copley Square, he used shape, orientation and mirrors to create the opposite effect. The distinctive rhomboid shape skews away from the Square and a vertical notch breaks its apparent mass.

The building's presence was erased from adjacent street views by its mirrored surfaced, regular fenestration pattern and lack of a unique facade for its three-storey street-level lobby. The reflections brilliantly negate the building's tectonic and mass at street level. Miraculously, the iconic sixty-two storey building has no existence at street grade, although approximately 100 feet from Trinity Church. When viewed from across the square on Boylston Street, the side facing Trinity Church appears as a mere 2D image, the rhomboid falls behind its St. James

11. Entrance to the Hancock Tower, Boston,
Architect Henry N. Cobb, I.M. Pei & Partners.
At street level, the building disappears.
© Bill Caplan

Avenue facade. Cobb achieved a nonintrusive interface for two million square feet of architecture (figures 11, 12 and 13). Yet at the same time, the Hancock Tower is an iconic presence.

12. The Hancock Tower's bulk (seen below) disappears behind its Copley Square face (left). © Bill Caplan

13. The Hancock Tower from
Clarendon Street (above);
the Stuart Street facade (right).
© Bill Caplan

14. The Seagram Building, Mies van der Rohe, New York. © Bill Caplan

Of course, making buildings disappear at street level is not the only way to render massive structures community-friendly. When designing New York City's Seagram Building (1958), Mies van der Rohe set it back from its property line to highlight its iconic form, creating a public plaza in front (Figure 14).

Mies sought visibility from street level, allowing the public to enjoy the entirety of the Seagram Building's architecture. This was an atypical tactic at a time when the city's high-rise buildings tended to hug the street line for their ten allowable storeys, greatly reducing pedestrian view of the architecture. Mies' people-friendly approach influenced the inclusion of incentives in New York's 1961 zoning code to encourage the development of public spaces in private buildings.

Its amber-tinted glass, although not mirrored, reflects the street scene (Figure 15). The Seagram Building does not disappear at street level, but integrates an ever-changing visual experience, a public-friendly presence.

Building envelopes like those of New York's Seagram Building and Boston's Hancock Tower visually respond to their local environments, reflecting images of nearby buildings, street life and nature. This light reflection, an operative property of the envelope that offers sensible experiences, is a quality of the architectural surface and substance.

15. The Seagram Building, Park Avenue entrance, New York. © Bill Caplan

Conversely, although it is an interesting sculptural form from afar, Frank Gehry's IAC building in New York City (2007) ignores human-friendly interfacing at street grade. One sees an irregular prismatic envelope of white fritted glass, a conspicuous visual and physical presence. Though dramatically visible from a distance, the effect is not readily accessible from close proximity or from within – either physically or cognitively. The white fritted curtain panels are so prominent that, in the absence of a setback from the building line on their narrow street, the panels seem encroaching, 'in your face'. With its sensible qualities limited to distant viewing, Gehry's design is not pedestrian friendly (figures 16 and 17).

16. The IAC Building, West Side Highway at 18th Street, NYC, Frank Gehry. © Bill Caplan

17. The IAC Building street interface on the West Side Highway. © Bill Caplan

While neither sidewalk friendly nor structural, the IAC's envelope admits and filters light, reflects rain, maintains a thermal differential and buffers the exterior environment. In these respects, its surface and substance provide a performative envelope, just as all buildings are performative in one way or another. The IAC envelope does not appear to be particularly notable in that regard, beyond the possibility of daylight or solar heat screening by its white glass frit.

► PERFORMATIVE INTERFACE – The Operative Presence of Architecture

Among the many notions of a building envelope, perhaps the most significant to the program, the wellbeing of the occupants and environmental sustainability is that of a *performative interface*. While shelter, program space and infrastructure arise from the material interfaces, and sense of place evolves from the experiential interfaces, program and environmental interactions develop from performative interfaces. They implement design performance and are *the key to 'green' design*.

From the performative perspective, the building envelope employs the functional qualities of a *substance*, a *membrane* and *technology* to enhance its programmatic and environmental efficacy. Technology might appear to be an outlier in this group; however, the functional technology of materials and their arrangement emerged millennia ago with building science. It is the technological *properties* of building components that are significant in this regard – what they afford, not the technology of building.

Since the late 1970s, significant advances in interface technology have become available to enhance the functionality of building components, broadening the very concept of material performance. Thus, a building envelope can be environmentally performative, aesthetically performative, energy interactive and even energy generative, or embody them all.

Physics, chemistry and sometimes biology determine the nature and flow of energy and material through an envelope's surfaces and substance. This includes optical, thermal, chemical, electrical and mechanical energies in the form of light, heat, airflow, sound and vibration.

18. Envelope screen on Royal Netherlands
Embassy Berlin, Rem Koolhass, OMA.
© Bill Caplan

The performative skin on Berlin's Royal Netherlands Embassy (Figure 18) mini-mises the public's view and the sun's heat with a perforated metal screen, yet admits light. Rain screens, exemplified in Figure 19, not only physically repel rain and winds from a building envelope, but vent pressure differentials capable of forcing water seepage though an envelope's seams. They also have an insulating effect and can contribute to the building's aesthetic.

19. Rain barrier tiles and ventilating sectors; a physical,
operative and sensible surface composite. Agrob Buchtal
Gmbh, designed by Herzog and de Meuron. 2014
Architecture Biennale, Venice. © Bill Caplan

Although building materials such as stone and concrete denote mass and structural qualities, their performative aspects extend beyond tectonics and physical
structure. Stone and concrete envelopes weather the exterior environment and

maintain thermal differentials by means of their physical properties and arrangement. They too are performative envelopes, as can be seen in the case of the Bahá'i House of Worship (1986), whose thermal and environmental qualities derive from the material selection and design configuration (Figure 20).

This ability to influence or utilise light, view, solar energy, water and wind, and to intake or exhaust air, heat and moisture, provides a large matrix of affordances – empowering architects and engineers with many opportunities to enhance twenty-first-century building. When we think of building interfaces as *interventional opportunities*, we can accomplish both people-friendly and environment-friendly building *by design*.

20. Bahá'i House of Worship, concrete and marble, New Dehli, India, Fariborz Sahba.
© Bill Caplan

We can model these physical and experiential interactions with a set of series and parallel algorithms, rule sets that orchestrate the change in energy and material flow from one surface through to the next – changes in environmental and experiential parameters between the exterior and the interior. Barriers and ports regulate these exchanges.

▶ BARRIERS AND PORTS – Selective Action

Employing any of the aforementioned perspectives – the physical, functional, cognitive or ecological – one can conceive a building envelope to be an assembly of *barriers* and *ports*. Envisioning this concept, one might think of walls, windows and doors, perhaps a roof, chimneys or vents – *enclosures, fenestration* and *access.*

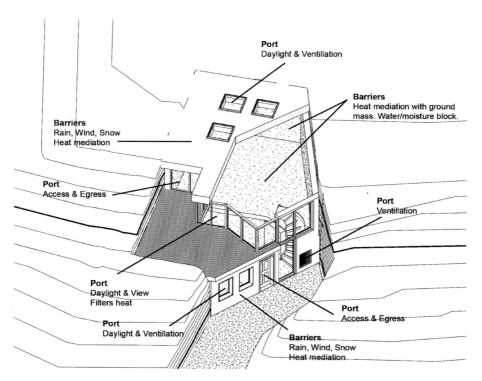

21. Envelope barriers and ports of an in-ground house (model by author).[12]
© Bill Caplan

46

The simple nomenclatures *window, wall, door, floor* and *roof* fail to express the breadth of affordance they offer – the enablement of a program and sense of place, enablements for the users and passersby, and symbioses with the environment. Barriers and ports are more than just building elements; they are functional interfacial means (Figure 21). While the purpose of an envelope barrier may be to restrict, restrain or demarcate, and a port's prime function to permit or transmit, their material properties afford other applications as well. In fact, although barriers prohibit, they also transmit both energy and matter; although ports allow passage, they also block.

Barriers Exclude Selectively

The barriers of a building envelope can create enclosure, separating one environment from another, such as exterior from interior. In the traditional sense, we speak of a wall, floor, ceiling, foundation or roof. Simplistically, they all block passage. Fortunately, there exist many other ways to bar or obstruct that can perform beneficial functions, such as to *reflect, scatter, direct* or *repel*. Buildings employ such affordances to achieve or reduce the in- or outflow of heat as with insulation, or as a barrier to water or moisture. These are selective measures of exclusion and prevention.

However, a barrier can also *absorb, filter, alter, reroute* or *eject* while achieving its primary purpose. Employing these means to redefine, direct or mediate the energy level inherent in heat, cold, wind, rain, light and any associated matter enhances the value of a building envelope significantly. A barrier can block the transfer of energy or an object completely, or alter the path, magnitude or rate of transfer. Reflecting, scattering, directing, absorbing, filtering, altering and ejecting *incident energy* offers many opportunities for both eco-sustainable design and human satisfaction.

Barrier components of the building envelope can serve multiple functions simultaneously – as elements of building enclosure *and* as *structures, energy storage wells, converters* or *generators*. In the hands of architects and engineers, they provide many physical and interfacial opportunities to selectively prohibit or mediate, functioning vectorially and/or generatively.

The outcome of every barrier interaction, whereby energy and/or matter act on the building envelope, results from the barrier's physical, chemical, electrical and mechanical properties. This provides a broad range of capabilities that can afford beneficial interactions throughout the spectrum of human ecological interfaces. Their materiality and arrangement can improve building performance as well as stimulate human perception – by design.

Ports Selectively Admit

Fenestrations of all sorts, the *ports* of the building envelope, serve to allow passage or transfer. Doors, windows and other openings permit the passage of energy and/ or matter. As with barriers, the actions afforded by ports have many degrees of subtlety.

A window typically enables the transmission of light, view and sometimes ventilation. Windows, portholes to the exterior, to other spaces and places, function according to their materials and makeup, such as the composition of their view panes. Although single, double and triple pane constructions can all transmit light and view, their thermal and noise transmission properties vary significantly. The composition of the panes themselves, whether glass or otherwise, the medium in between or the employment of screens, brises-soleil, light shelves, vents, surface coatings or thermal breaks likewise determine their performance. The manner in which ports function depends on the selection of materials, texture, technology, layering, shape, form and layout.

As with barriers, ports can transmit, reflect, scatter, direct, absorb, filter, alter or generate energy. Nevertheless, they operate in conjunction with their primary function to enable passage. They can mediate solar or ambient light and light emitted or reflected from objects, people, animals and the environment. Ports can mediate heat, sound or vibration as well as induce or filter the flow and exchange of air. They can employ a door, hatch, forced airflow or pressure, double or multiple skins or a void with no skin at all. Shading devices, deflectors, wavelength filters and energy-generating films can greatly augment their efficacy. Ports emphasise access – uninhibited or selective. They too are versatile building components in the hands of the architect or engineer, able to stimulate human perception and improve performance through design.

Barriers Can Be Ports; Ports Can Be Barriers

Every element of the envelope, whether a barrier or a port, can be designed to serve multiple functions, can simultaneously serve several uses. Opportunity is the point. Rather than treat each building component solely in terms of its primary function, leaving its other interfacial interactions to happenstance, we can design them to proactively augment other performance characteristics of the envelope.

Embodied as One

Apple's flagship store on Fifth Avenue in Manhattan (2006) in figures 22 and 23 is an interesting example that redefines the conventional understanding of a building envelope and its components. Bohlin Jackson's creation employs a single

22. Glass walls, roof, structure: Apple Store by Bohlin Jackson, Fifth Avenue, New York City.
© Bill Caplan

23. Glass stairs and elevator, Apple Store,
Fifth Avenue, New York City.
© Bill Caplan

material for structure, enclosure, barriers, ports and circulation – glass. A single
envelope material embodies all of these characteristics simultaneously, as structural support, wall, roof, door, window or stairs. Apple's Fifth Avenue building
functions as a physical, cognitive and performative envelope combined.

Vittorio Garatti's never-completed National Ballet School of Cuba (1961) also
evinces this phenomenon. Constructed with local brick and terra cotta using
the Catalan vault structural method, it is another example in which one element
marries the physical, cognitive and performative envelopes. The cladding and
structure are one; in this case brick (Figure 24).

24. Cuban National Arts School in Havana by Vittorio Garatti. © Bill Caplan

From an interfacial perspective, the components of a building envelope can be selectively impenetrable or permeable to various forms of energy and matter, controlling such transmission. This holds for both barriers and ports, which often serve multiple functions simultaneously. For example, fenestration that ports light and view can serve as a barrier to wind and rain. Likewise, a wall barring the passage of people, weather and light, can be fashioned to minimise the undesirable transmission of sound and heat or cold. Barriers and ports can be designed to serve multiple functions. While deliberately serving in their primary physical, operative or experiential roll, they can equally contribute additional people-friendly and 'green' characteristics.

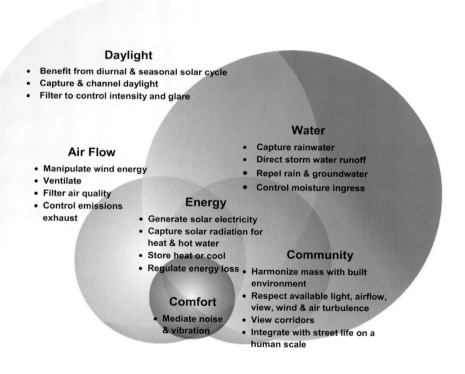

Daylight
- Benefit from diurnal & seasonal solar cycle
- Capture & channel daylight
- Filter to control intensity and glare

Water
- Capture rainwater
- Direct storm water runoff
- Repel rain & groundwater
- Control moisture ingress

Air Flow
- Manipulate wind energy
- Ventilate
- Filter air quality
- Control emissions exhaust

Energy
- Generate solar electricity
- Capture solar radiation for heat & hot water
- Store heat or cool
- Regulate energy loss

Community
- Harmonize mass with built environment
- Respect available light, airflow, view, wind & air turbulence
- View corridors
- Integrate with street life on a human scale

Comfort
- Mediate noise & vibration

25. A few barrier and port design capabilities.

3 *People*

"I have now to deal only with the sensible impressions,
which no book or picture can give."

Goethe, September 1776[13]

► THE HUMAN EXPERIENCE –
Visual, Corporeal and Cognitive

Buildings are for people. Materiality and arrangement afford cognitive perception, experiential attributes that can *imply* mass and space, past and future, safe harbour or risk, tonality and tonicity, purpose, personality and affectations – attributes that can evoke visceral responses. The *sensible qualities* of a building's physical embodiment provide experiential context.

Buildings come to mind as places with or without our first-hand corporeal experience. We often perceive the nature of a building from visual clues before participating in corporeal interaction. Visual expression is a component of the building's *experiential interface*. Of course, we interpret this visual interaction in conjunction with the other sensory clues available, as well as innate instinct and prior experience.

Articulation of a building's visual character is multilingual and multi-syntactical, and is expressed by shape, texture, colour and the qualities of solids, liquids and/ or gases. Form, arrangement and volumetric constraints are only some of the visual characteristics that emanate; light and shadow resolve them as mass and voids that demark space and enclose place. A building's physical envelope manifests an architectural tectonic, but its *visual perception emerges in the context of its surroundings and those of its viewer.*

One's first visual encounter embraces the overall character of the envelope or the portion in focus. The fundamental form coalesces cognitively before the details emerge. This interaction with architecture, the perception of shape and form, narrows to a glimpse of a portion of the building's exterior.

The material/mechanical assemblies that comprise *a building's surfaces enrich our conception of its physicality.* Forged to fit pre-determined boundaries, the surface, punctuated by apertures and voids, enunciates the architectural composition. Nevertheless, from the viewer's perspective, it is the tectonic that defines these limits, not the reverse – the building defines the space, the space does not define the building. *The viewer conjures the viewer's tectonic;* it is a cognitive perception.

Together, tectonic organisation and material composition project a building's presence to the community and passersby (Figure 26); however, this is only a representation, a visual interface.

Coloured by prior experience and memory, the building we perceive evokes associations, but lacks corporeal sensation beyond those visceral or emotively induced, merely projecting an effect. Yet even without the aid of prior personal experience or the corporeal interactions of touch, smell, taste or sound, we perceive the character of shape, organisation, materiality and relative dimensions, an ephemeral vision.

As we approach, its spatial and material qualities formulate. Light conditions, weather, season, time of day, ambient noise, the presence of people and one's mood all add tone.

Although we may stop momentarily for a mental snapshot, our interaction with architecture is a dynamic experience, viewed in movement – walking, running, perhaps from an escalator or a vehicle. It is an analogue event, a continuous experience of ever-changing sequential views; alternately expansive or precisely targeted (Figure 27).

26. Passing the Guggenheim Bilbao,
Frank Gehry. © Bill Caplan

Our visual perception of architecture occurs from the perspective of locomotion, transference, random eye movement or intentional focus. In *Thinking, Fast and Slow (2011)*, Daniel Kahneman reminds: "Whenever your eyes are open, your brain computes a three-dimensional representation of what is in your field of vision, complete with the shape of objects, their position in space, and their identity. No intention is needed to trigger this operation or the continuous monitoring for violated expectations."[14]

The way we perceive sensory inputs makes architecture both experiential and personal. A true evaluation of architecture requires an interactive experience from multiple perspectives. Its representation in a drawing, photograph or computer rendering can be meaningful only in tandem with experiencing the fundamental characteristics that form its essence. The near and far, inside and out, wide angle and detail, light and shade and darkness, texture and tactility, sound and scent – all inform the mind's eye, all cull our emotional sense. Clear or cloudy skies, wind, rain and the seasons colour our impression, as does one's perspective as spectator or occupant, alone or with others. Experiences like these determine how we *see* architecture and, hence, its viability.

Each of us experiences the world uniquely. Taste and preference are personal qualities that stem from a complex interaction of parameters that span genetics, culture, upbringing, physical characteristics, body chemistry, the environment, one's occupation, friendships and many other influences and conditioners. Yet we all share innate instincts that drive our species plus a sensory/cognitive system to receive and process information. The world perceived through our senses comes to life through this corporeal electro-chemical biological system.

We possess five senses with which to assimilate our surroundings and a brain to interpret them, to create consciousness, time and manage our interventions. Quite naturally, this is how we experience the built environment. Understanding the instincts and mechanisms that drive our consciousness, how we see, sense and instinctively relate to the world, and how we react physically and emotionally to the elements of architecture, aids the creation of a human ecological design. As architecture is created for people, all those involved in its design must be conscious of its human interface; *experiential context drives human ecological design.*

What We See and How We Perceive It – More than Meets the Eye

People experience the architectural envelope through the human envelope, our *physical, sensible and operative interface* with the universe. Facilitated by an exterior skin integrated with a sensory/cognitive system, an active mechanical structure enhances our personal interface. Continuously monitored by the brain, our sensory receptors respond to changing light, pressure, temperature, chemistry and electrical charge. The human envelope is analogous to the building envelope in many ways; it is environmentally permeable and mediates exchanges of matter and energy with its outer and inner worlds. Interestingly, our perception of both envelopes, built and human, is a product of the human mind. *Reality derives from perception.*

Cognitive psychologist Chris Frith writes in *Making Up the Mind: How the Brain Creates our Mental World (2007)* that "Our perception of the world is a fantasy that coincides with reality."[15] The world we know is the world our brain creates, perceived with the aid of our sensory system. We interpret it in a perpetual loop of experiential knowledge biased by instinctual preferences. Our perception of architecture is no exception. Formed through *personal* interactions and biases, our experience is not necessarily that of the architect.

Nonetheless, although people experience phenomena differently, our receptors, body and brain possess the same functional modes to process similar inputs. Reality may be personal, yet for composite identities, it is remarkably similar to the reality of others. A tree is a tree to most people who see one. This would seem obvious. However, consider the numerous components that compose an image projected on the retina. There are a multitude of possible combinations, associations and interpretations of its shapes, shadows, colourations, textures, lines and forms – all in motion.[16]

With this instinctual cognitive–sensory process, informed by learning and context, we experience the grandness of nature, the perception of power, and forces of the physical universe. Through it, we experience the feelings of energy and awe that can stimulate, comfort, overwhelm or intrigue us, and that instil feelings of respect, wellbeing or fear. We experience architecture through this same process. Present experience references the past while anticipating the future. Expectation has a significant role in this process. *Our relationship with architecture is always experiential.*

Mental images are contextual, interpreted in the contexts of our entire interaction, not just our visual impressions. We understand them in concert with our memories and powers of perception that incorporate gravity, balance, temperature and electrical charge as well as the corporeal senses of hearing, touch, smell and taste. The visual envelope is experiential, physically and cognitively conceived in terms of our five senses in a three-dimensional framework and time. The articulation of form and organisation acquires new meaning when enhanced by knowledge of a building's plan and circulation, spatial volumes, lighting, medium, textures, sounds, scents and use. Cognition nurtures the experience fabricated by our mind's eye.

Whether experienced from an exterior or interior perspective, *architecture defines the immediate environment*, evoking a sense of place. The opera house in Oslo (Figure 28) becomes an urban park, a landscape; Berlin's Paul-Löbe-Haus streetscape (Figure 29) becomes an event. They are interacting experiences.

We experience the language of architecture – the language of mass, void, light and shadow. The syntax, based in shape, proportion and its articulation, whether primitive form or a complex expression of form and light, can impart emotive sensations to human perception, such as the awe provoked in cathedrals (Figure 30).

Daniel Libeskind's Jewish Museum Berlin and Peter Eisenman's Berlin Memorial to the Murdered Jews of Europe demonstrate this correlation between the expressive language of form and our physical state of being. A simple walk through these architectural works physically disorients. One perceives the experience emotionally as well as physically, largely due to the orientation and juxtapositions of shape, mass and void, as well as perspective, floor gradient, texture and light.

30. El Transparente altarpiece,
thirteenth-century Cathedral of Saint
Mary, Toledo, Spain. © Bill Caplan

29. Paul-Löbe-Haus forum facing the
Berlin Chancellery, Stephen Braunfels
Architekten. © Bill Caplan

31. Jewish Museum Berlin, Studio Daniel Libeskind.
© Bill Caplan

The use of narrow view corridors, overpowering height to width ratios, sloped floors and ceilings, irregular fenestration, light and shadow, maze-like paths, quiet or distant sounds, irregular ground surface and obstacles, heighten the senses betraying expectations and balance. Masterfully accomplished, the emotive impact significantly magnifies the conscious emotions one experiences relating to the Holocaust that they memorialise. The language of architecture is experiential – it is interactive (figures 31 and 32).

32. Memorial to the Murdered Jews of Europe, Berlin, Eisenman Architects. © Bill Caplan

Visual characteristics often evoke an experiential response through cause and effect associations. We respond to form and shape emotionally, emotion and perception intertwine. Expressed by neuropsychologist Richard Gregory, "Emotions can affect perception... perceptions can affect emotion."[17] Our tendency to perceive relationships, form conclusions and anticipate events associates our emotive responses to the world we experience – our perception of form, shape, orientation and sequential events.

To Pritzker Laureate Peter Zumthor, "Our perception is visceral. Reasons play a secondary role."[18] Our perceptions of sound, smell, taste, touch and the effects of gravity form experiences, and indeed provoke visceral responses – emotions, feelings or a consciousness attuned to joy or sorrow, love, hate or fear. Emotion is *a mental state that is experienced*. The reality of architecture is a human response, a figment of brain processing – more than geometry and physical substance, and more than meets the eye alone. To design for people is to acknowledge the phenomena to which we respond.

▶ VISUALISATION –
We See with the Mind's Eye

Having the ability to target, change focus and adjust resolution with incredible accuracy and speed, the mind's eye is a wondrous creation of the brain. Scanning enables us to visualise a broad view, include peripheral vision, frame the focus on specific objects or extract fine detail. In less than the blink of an eye, it captures the entirety of a painting as well as the detail of the brushstrokes. It is able to detect visual associations of other physical inputs, such as temperature, sound or tactility, imaging ephemera as elusive as heat waves in the air or the blur of vibration. Seeing, which means visualising in the cognitive context, is a "constructive process"[19]; the brain's assumptions and fabrications, based on prior experience, intellectualise what we see.

Eyes sense and decode light. They are sensitive to incoming images composed of varying intensities and wavelengths projected over millions of light and motion activated photoreceptive cells of the retina. Yet we visualise things cognitively, *experiencing* more than the eye sees. What a person sees is not the reassembly of pixilated imagery, but a visualisation that draws from our entire sensory system, as well as memory – the conscious and the subconscious. As expressed by neuroscientist Eric Kandel, "the eye does not work like a camera"[20], vision is an interpretation of the mind.

Integral to this process, the mind makes assumptions and fills in missing pieces – not always correctly. The *mind's eye* is a visual-to-cognitive interface empowered by the entirety of the sensory and cognitive systems. The numerous specialty sensors forming the retina parse characteristics of the two-dimensional images focused there by the eye's lens. Activated in real time, each of these retina cells initiates a signal to the brain.

Some cells are highly reactive to *lines* and *edges* or *preferred orientations* of lines, edges or moving patterns.[21] Some neuron responses depend on the movement of an object relative to its background.[22] As a result, we respond well to line orientation, pattern orientation and directional movement; we sense horizontal, vertical and lines that are oblique. We respond best to boundaries between light and dark, which enable us to discern edges.[23]

Light and colour detection also carry an emotive impact. Kandel notes in *The Age of Insight* (2012) that colours add to the value of form's perception. In the same manner that we perceive facial expression before its identity, *we perceive an object's colour before its form* or before we perceive its motion.[24] He concludes that "our brain processes aspects of the image that relate to emotional perception more rapidly than aspects that relate to form, thus setting the emotional tone for the form – the object or the face – confronting us."[25]

Nevertheless, these corresponding signals to the brain do *not* form a visualised 'picture' from the light pattern projected alone. Other receptors that sense hearing, touch, taste and smell, and phenomena such as time, temperature and gravity, add qualities. In conjunction with contemporaneous associations and memory, the brain synthesises the 3D world, associating these events with shapes, relationships and other symbols, coloured by prior experience and innate instincts. *The brain creates the scene*, selectively authoring the visual continuum generating new inputs to our sense of being and memory.

The most significant associations we perceive, those that evoke energy, emotion or wellbeing, can enhance the effectiveness of architecture. They are capable of instilling emotional or physical stimulation or a sense of security in architecture's reality.

Human perception bridges the physical world and our emotional and physical response, often to something inferred – a cognitive link between what we see and how we feel or act. We experience this phenomenon in our palpable relationship to attraction, repulsion and gravity vectors. Even the location of a spot on an otherwise blank page can viscerally provoke an attraction.

Attractors

The striking use of texture, light, colour or exaggerated features can activate the brain's amygdala, an integral part of the system for processing emotions such as pleasure and fear. Such activations link to physiological and unconscious response.[26] We can see this in the power of Roni Horn's glasswork: its light energy draws the viewer with an incredible intensity (Figure 33).

Just as we anticipate the future action of a pendulum's swing or a ball's bounce, even a static mass tempting gravity or a discontinuity tempting fracture suggests their course. Perceiving the presence of energy, such as forces of attraction, repulsion, the gravity of objects and their arrangement or the containment of light, we allude to a cognitive impression. Without an input from a time-related event, we can still sense a potential, a cognitive expectation – *anticipation* – thereby magnifying the nature of the sensation.

These sensations can convey a premonition, an implication of consequences and an immediate future, a dynamic continuity in time. We can experience emotive and physiological *sensations created by the mind*, not just by physical inputs to our sensory system.

In *A Dynamic Systems Approach to the Development of Cognition and Action*, Thelan and Smith explain: "Patterns of repeated activity over time become stable attractors. Thus, particular configurations of activity at one moment in time generate future activity."[27] In other words, associations or events that we have repeatedly

33. Solid cast glass by Roni Horn, Punta della Dogana, Venice. © Bill Caplan

gathered in our knowledge base will cause that experience to be expected – an attracting trajectory[28] of our anticipated experience.

Suggesting a future state from the present visual or sensory context, or energy's perceived containment, release or existence, can initiate a trajectory of cognitive momentum. We factor perception with our understanding of time. *Time gives 'meaning' a trajectory*. Cognitive momentum that we perceive from the energy of shape and form can generate attractors.

To Gregory, our cognitive ability to anticipate a trajectory forward is vital to our existence, "employing knowledge stored from the past, to see the present and predict the immediate future. Prediction has immense survival value."[29] This perception of both past and future is an association conceived as a continuum, inherent in contemporaneously experienced objects or circumstances. It relates to our intuitive understanding and cumulative knowledge of how energy behaves. Anticipation and expectation are not only functions of what is forthcoming – cognitive momentum – but also of what exists now. Anticipation is a significant factor in the human interface, one that influences wellbeing.

Attractors in architecture create trajectories, they can peak curiosity and instil anticipation. Architectural attractors can emerge from the simple orchestration of shapes and form as demonstrated in works by Zaha Hadid and Carlo Scarpa in figures 34 and 35.

34. Trajectory attractors: Piranesian stairs at the Maxxi museum, Rome, Zaha Hadid. © Bill Caplan

35. Trajectory attractors: portals at Castelvecchio, Carlo Scarpa's intervention, Verona. © Bill Caplan

Illusions

Our experiential interactions with architecture often include illusions, sometimes simply aiding the understanding of what we see by filling in missing pieces, or perceiving an effect intended by the architect.

The perception of form develops quickly as we process the relationships between outlines and shape. Once experienced, shape becomes a cognitive presence in memory, a constituent of knowledge. Thus embedded, the mind can recall or complete a shape perceiving only part of its outline.

Francis Crick, co-discoverer of the structure of the DNA molecule, believed that a group of retinal neurons responding to line *length* or *termination* might contribute to our perception of *illusory contours,* lines that we perceive but do not actually exist in the visual image seen.[30] Combined with experiential knowledge, these lines and contours often signify an object, recalled from memory. Notice the white triangle in Figure 36, the well-known Kanizsa triangle: it is a figure of the mind.

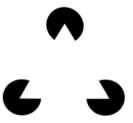

36. Memory suggests shape (Kanizsa triangle).[31]

The line terminations in Figure 37 frame the same illusory shape; it is a false perception. The retina's versatility and sensitivity is complex.

37. Illusory triangle from line terminations.[32]

The mind attempts to fulfil one's expectation, providing missing or unseen pieces to complete physical shapes. This produces interesting effects, such as interpolating curves and contours between misaligned edges, visualising *illusionary contours* where they do not exist.[33]

38. Illusory inflected contours on three sides of the triangle.

Notice the different contours discernible in the three sides of the distorted illusionary Kanizsa triangle in Figure 38. One sees inflected contours completing the triangle instead of straight lines, creations of the mind based on cumulative expectations. Our visualisation of the knotted marble in Figure 39 is formed in the same manner.

39. Illusion of entwined marble, twelfth-century
Modena Cathedral, Italy. © Bill Caplan

40. We are aware of the fourth support without
seeing it. National Ballet School of Cuba,
awaiting reconstruction, 2013. © Bill Caplan

These illusions help us visualise architecture; our mind's eye completes the lines,
curvatures, contours and missing pieces for components we see in partial view, or
during locomotion (Figure 40).

▶ ENERGY, MATTER AND PEOPLE –
The Human Response

Energy and matter are the minimal requirements necessary to sustain all living species. Effectively interchangeable, energy and matter are life's building blocks, the key to procreation. Even the processes of sensing and thinking require energy to stimulate receptors and to store, recall and process thoughts. Both our corporeal and cognitive systems require continuous energy consumption to function.

Responding to such primordial needs, we instinctively perceive energy indicators in both phenomena and matter. As a species, we cannot succeed without them. The biological imperative to sustain life and replicate not only relies on the pursuit of energy and elemental matter, but also on the availability of shelter for self-preservation and energy conservation. Thus emerged the quest to control our environment, the impetus for human-centric design.

Neurobiologist John M. Allman points out that "Mammals expend most of their energy maintaining a constant body temperature."[34] This is an important point, one that draws us to shelter. This corporeal imperative, not only benefits from energy's *availability*, but also from the *efficiency* of its use and the efficacy of its *conservation*. As such, we are motivated to seek shelter, a means to conserve energy through containment, insulation and the regulation of airflow, all of which assist temperature regulation.

Mankind's need for a built environment starts with this imperative for survival, the drive to enhance our circumstances in the unforgiving natural environment we depend upon. The environment we build, the natural environment and the imprint of human activity are competing realities. The outcome of that competition is highly dependent on the ecological sensitivity of our designs. More than just sustaining our natural resources, it also entails the *human aspect* of ecology, an individual's human interface, one's personal physical and mental wellbeing.

Exploring the character of the human response to energy and matter is a good place to begin. Attention to the way we perceive stimuli and respond to energy is an important element of successful design. *Energy* is life's animating force and a key to animating architecture.

Anticipation: Energy Evokes a Visceral Response

Animals in the wild are attracted to salt licks to maintain electrolytic balance in their body fluids. They sense the presence of salt, a learning process driven by instinct. In a similar way, we learn to detect the properties of energy, specific signs of its presence and source, correlating these sensations with energy propinquity. We attribute them to physical expressions of energy or its containment. This may be manifest in immediate sensations as with heat, light, sound or gravity; or in recognition of its past presence – such as hearing thunder after lightening, or with a fracture or cleft on the verge of failure.

What is it about shape and form, when expressed by surface texture, angles, cracks, crevices, fragmentation, asymmetries, imperfections and organic matter, that peaks our interest or interacts with human perception? *We visually perceive their energy.*

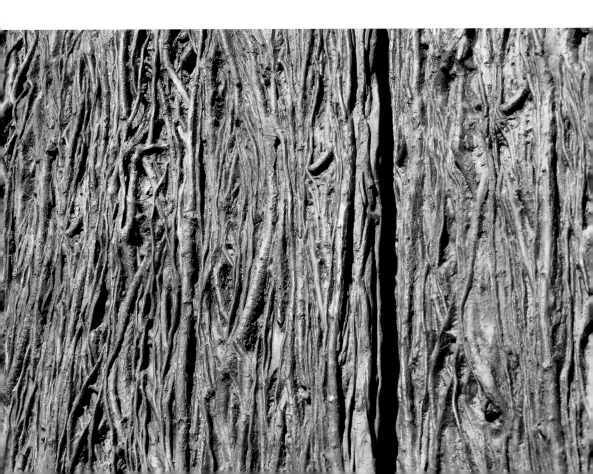

41. Dense woody vegetation cast as
bronze doors, evoking visceral sensations
of growth and energy entanglement.
Cristina Iglesias 2007, Museo del Prado,
Madrid. © Bill Caplan

42. Visual signs of a prior event evoke
sensations of energy flow – embodied
here in form, crystallisation and rupture.
Lava formation on Fernandina Island,
Galapagos. © Bill Caplan

The same applies to a long list of cognitively linked sensibilities that associate energy to irregularities such as imbalance, asymmetry, creases, folds, bubbles, ripples, flow lines and stratifications. Whether frozen in stone, embodied in growth or dynamic in a fluid, these indicators reveal energy's past or presence versus time: energy stored, energy spent or energy in action. We sense this in creations of nature and in their artistic representations (figures 41 and 42).

Awareness of energy's magnitude is so important to our survival that *we learn to anticipate* its potential – a mound of sand one grain's weight from collapse, an avalanche awaiting minimal force to trigger destruction, an iceberg near rupture, a slowly moving glacier – latency on the verge of kinetic release (figures 43, 44 and 45).

We perceive the energy of gravity, even when merely implied. Stand under a large overhanging rock, walk close to Richard Serra's giant skewed steel slab, picnic at the edge of a cliff, look up at a balanced boulder or the lean of Pisa's Tower: the energy is palpable, sometimes disorienting (Figure 46).

In some cases, energy is stored – awaiting or straining to release – in others, it is illusionary: mental or physical anticipation, recognition of characteristic signs. We innately comprehend the importance of energy, a source of life that can be healthy, rejuvenating and stimulating to the senses. Conversely, the lack of energy can convey stagnancy, sickness or ill health. Energy can overpower and destroy, not only in a pulse of large magnitude, but through minor incremental applications. A small change in equilibrium can release a catastrophic response.

The significance of latent and potential energy resides in our subconscious, associated with prior knowledge gleaned from experiences. Kinetic energy lives in a present conscious moment; its actions, synthesised by our perception, also imprint our memory. We *associate* this knowledge with physical shapes, orientation and inferences of their history; they connect us to the physical world and the world of architecture – a connection both spatial and emotive.

Landscape architect Lawrence Halprin described this interplay between energy, environment and design:

> Nature has many lessons for us, but to me, as a designer, these two are most important. The first of these is that order, natural order, is overwhelmingly clear and that I relate to it easily and organically and my own sense of order derives from it.
>
> ...This order has to do with process – it has to do with natural rhythms, of qualities of relationships between objects; of lightness and heaviness; of the sense of gravity and the density of rock, of energy and force.[35]

43. Latent energy, unstable rock scree slide, Spitsbergen, Svalbard Archipelago. © Bill Caplan

44. Iceberg on the verge of rupture, Lago Grey Peninsula, Patagonia. © Bill Caplan

45. Approaching glacial flow, Beagle Channel, Tierra del Fuego. © Bill Caplan

46. Torre di
Pisa, Italy.
© Bill Caplan

We depend on energy in numerous forms to support life; among them, it is the means by which our senses receive stimulation and transmit to the brain, and the means by which we think. We effortlessly associate with energy, a component of all things physical and mental – as such, *energy is a component of architecture*.

Shape and Form: We Sense Energy in Material Things

Interactions between the built environment and our ecosystem are often apparent; the links between buildings and people can be less clear. A building's human dimensions entail two aspects – one relates to a building's program and the people who participate, the other relates to its emotive and visceral effect on human activity, productivity, health and happiness. These too derive from interactions among people, matter and energy, but in a different way; they emanate from the qualities and relationships of material shape and form. The envelope of shape, its angles and curvature, inflection, continuity and texture, expresses energy in ways to which we relate. *Material things embody energy*.

> The Architect, by his arrangement of forms, realizes an order which is a pure crea-
> tion of his spirit; by forms and shapes he affects our senses to an acute degree
> and provokes plastic emotions; by the relationships which he creates he wakes
> profound echoes in us, he gives us the measure of an order which we feel to be in
> accordance with that of our world, he determines the various movements of our
> heart and of our understanding; it is then that we experience the sense of beauty.
>
> Le Corbusier[36]

Our associations to form, shape and arrangement are strong. For thousands of years philosophers have empowered them with the essence of spiritual and meta-physical context, as in the practice of *feng shui*.

As early as the second century BC, the feng shui school of Form (Landform) incorporated principles based on fundamental relationships entwining form and its life energy, *ch'i*. Feng Shui Master Shan-Tung Hsu, PhD explains:

> In Chinese metaphysics, ch'i is the very essence or element that composes the
> whole universe. All forms, all manifestations, come from ch'i. Without ch'i,
> there would be no universe. Once the universe appears, all its transformations
> and developments are nothing but the transformations between ch'i and form…
> When there is no ch'i, living beings die, and material forms disintegrate.[37]

If we equate form to matter and matter to mass, energy – the essence of the metaphysical ch'i – brings to mind the recently confirmed Higgs field and its corresponding Higgs boson, through which nuclear particles acquire mass. In feng shui, "Form defines energy, and energy manifests through form."[38] The application of its fundamental principles relies on the interrelationship of the cognitive perception of form and our physiological response. We perceive this energy directly.[39]

> When you look at these forms, do you have different reactions? Most likely, you will feel a difference between them, though you may not be able to say clearly what it is. These forms have a physiological or psychological impact, below or beyond the level of ordinary awareness. ...think about three dimensional objects, like a cube or sphere. Their impact is even more definite.[40]

Perceiving energy, we formulate associations – experiential processing begins. As Vincent Scully expressed it, "There is no way to separate form from meaning; one cannot exist without the other."[41] To Scully, it is only a matter of the ways "through which form transmits meaning to the viewer." To Peter Zumthor, the way is the spark, energy's transmission, the "sensation of beauty is not ignited by the form as such but rather by the spark that jumps from it to me."[42]

Form is a "Diagram of Forces" – An Inextricable Link Between a Volume and Energy

Relating form and growth to physical laws and mathematics in his 1917 book *On Growth and Form*, the biologist D'Arcy Wentworth Thompson posited that the shape and characteristics of form imply a relationship to "the action of force", to the energy of formation.

> The form, then, of any portion of matter, whether it be living or dead, and the changes of form that are apparent in its movements and in its growth, may in all cases alike be described as due to the action of force. In short, the form of an object is a "diagram of forces" in this sense, at least, that from it we can judge of or deduce the forces that are acting or have acted upon it: in this strict and particular sense, it is a diagram, – in the case of a solid, of the forces that *have* been impressed upon it when its conformation was produced,

together with those that enable it to retain its conformation; in the case of a liquid (or of a gas) of the forces that are for the moment acting on it to restrain or balance its own inherent mobility.

...Now the state, including the shape or form, of a portion of matter, is the resultant of a number of forces, which represent or symbolize the manifestations of various kinds of energy...[43]

Thompson addressed shape and form in the broad sense, not only through the structure of cells or crystals, but by comparing phenomena such as the spherical surface of raindrops and oceans. A raindrop's shape results from surface energy (surface tension), the ocean's surface from gravity (a form of mass energy). Likewise, surface tension governs water ripples; gravity governs large waves.[44]

We need not know why or how particular shapes form to sense their energy content: we sense it from learned associations. We *perceive* the energy's presence and sometimes its relative magnitude – not in a quantitative way, but in an associative way. We sense this influence simply from shape and form, although we may not articulate that knowledge. Architecturally, shape results from matter and void, substance subtracted, mass added or growth within a void – each an embodiment of energy or its interface. Their gestures, those that stimulate visceral or emotive impact, draw from our instincts and experiences, such as the effects of gravity, or precarious relationships, force fields, physical failure, erosion, decay and the massive, minimal or flimsy. Through experiential imprinting and conditioning, energetic shapes and their interfacial containers enrich us mentally and physically. We discern propitious as well as ominous shapes – they embody energy.

Indicators

Indicators of energy emerge at stages of relative simplicity, at or near their asymmetrical tipping point or vector reversal, places of inflection, singularities, or maximum or minimum curvature. They interact with other forces or energy indicators in the environment. Thompson pointed out that intricate complexity starts simply, resulting from comparatively simple intrinsic system forces interacting with simple forces of the surrounding medium:

> If we blow into a bowl of soapsuds and raise a great mass of many-hued and variously shaped bubbles, if we explode a rocket and watch the regular and beautiful configuration of its falling streamers, if we consider the wonders of a limestone cavern which a filtering stream has filled with stalactites, we soon perceive that in all these cases we have begun with an initial system of very slight complexity, whose structure in no way foreshadowed the result, and whose comparatively simple intrinsic forces only play their part by complex interaction with the equally simple forces of the surrounding medium.[45]

Energy indicators are an *inherent* property of the element's shape, form or presence.

The mere existence of an object, its presence in our field of vision, provokes cognitive actions that subconsciously note its characteristic components, searching for prior experiential associations. This continuous process arouses our perception of their energy value or influence. The human brain processes object relationships in dialogue with memory, coloured by instinct. Shape, orientation and juxtaposition frame both our perception of the physical world and our experiential connection to architecture. Experienced as emotive and visceral responses in addition to a physical sensation, energy perceived in the built environment influences human activity, productivity, health and happiness. *Energy content is an important component* of architecture's human value.

Appreciating this interaction of mind and object, allowing it to influence the creative process, is fundamental to achieving a human ecological design.

Everything contains energy – objects as well as thought formation. Shapes, forms and compositions express this energy, reflect this energy – we relate to it. Energy fields reside between objects and our cognitive perception and in their mutual relationships. We perceive this energy. We perceive it in the relationships of architecture and the built environment as well.

A simple mark in an otherwise blank space demonstrates this point. A dot on a page is a location, a symbol, a component – it has substance, provides focus and contributes to the expression of energy. The addition of a single point to what was otherwise a blank space creates an attractor; cause for energetic eye-movement and energy flow within the brain.

A single dot energises an empty space. Does the dot to the right distract you?   ●

It defines the spatial coordinates. The dot embodies simplicity, from which complexity can spring. Its mere existence activates the human mind.

Visually discernible, its physicality implies either mass-energy or the application of energy. A physical thing itself, it has shape.

A point's existence embodies energy and so does its relationship with the surroundings, which tethers the point to its context.

Forces activate between one point or object and another. They actuate meaning, location or vector direction, even communication. Each relationship evokes mental energy in the viewer. A single point matters – it can energise or catalyse.

Adjacency and Proximity: We Sense Energy in Arrangement

The visual phenomena that drive neural activity have evolved in conjunction with our instinctive relationship to energy. Visual perception not only entwines intimately with sensing energy, but with its packaging as well. Although shape and form by themselves project a manifestation of energy, adjacency and proximity often invoke a sense of its scalar or vector influence. We innately comprehend the energy of gravitational fields, such as the forces on the Leaning Tower of Pisa in Figure 46, but also realise the energy effects in magnetic and force fields from experience.

Repulsion, attraction and gravity vectors – operators for these fields – are part of our knowledge base, part of a natural order. They express and carry energy. Through them, we perceive the potential energy inherent in closely situated objects, as if one were encroaching on the other's boundary or their fields were building in strength. All of these drive our unconscious perception of architectural form and mass, and their relationship to the built and natural environments. Not only the shape and form of things but also their *adjacency and proximity impart a sense of energy* that we perceive.

47. Intertwining spans create a sphere of influence, Passerelle Simone-de-Beauvoir, Paris, Dietmar Feichtinger. © Bill Caplan

48. Passerelle Simone-de-Beauvoir, Paris,
Dietmar Feichtinger. © Bill Caplan

Object juxtaposition can intimate a sphere of influence, as with the intertwining bridge spans in figures 47 and 48. Energy is inherent in our perception
of the interplay of shapes and forms, both as an instinctual and a conditioned
response.

Objects askew in an asymmetrical position promote a sense of pressure or tension, repulsion or attraction. The centred dot in the upper frame of Figure 49 provides a sense of balance. Skewed toward the upper-right corner in the lower frame, the dot is no longer in balance. Proximate to the frame's corner, the dot now relates with the frame, creating a sense of tension, of direction, of vectors. Proximity to an edge or to another object, or an imbalance, generates a magnified perception of energy, activating the sense of an energy field.

49. Skewing the dot proximate to the edge increases energy.

The same applies to lines and edges, which we perceive in relation to gravity as well as relational orientations. The skewed line in Figure 50 implies significantly more energy than would a horizontal line.

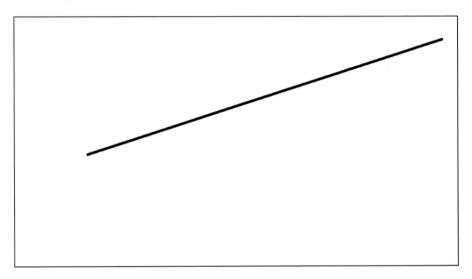

50. Skewing the line increases energy.

We even notice when objects are only slightly askew. For some people, a meagre half-degree tilt of a wall hanging requires straightening.

We subconsciously relate symmetry to balance, imbalance to gravity, and the proximity of nearness to attractive or repulsive fields. Well wired, we visualise not only shape, position and depth, but also *alignment* relating to gravity and other energy vectors, parameters relating to the perception of level, imbalance and implied force.

Although we tend to focus attention on a specific object or task, many ancillary events and conditions attract our conscious or subconscious attention. These events or conditions are *attractors*, or sometimes more appropriately distractors. They can add interesting nuance to unconscious interpretation, to desirability. We see beauty in proportion and symmetry, yet asymmetry and irregularity attract our attention. We notice a crack, crevice, fragmentation, shock or surprise; they are implications of a discontinuous occurrence, of an energy event or energy contained. They alert us. Why did they occur, what was the trigger, how will it evolve; most importantly, what is its energy factor – the *human attractor* factor?

51. Villa Savoye, Corbusier, 1931.
© Isabelle Lomholt

What are the attractors that empower the design of Corbusier's Villa Savoye in Figure 51? Rather than the style or principles of the modern 'movement', its simplicity of form, asymmetric juxtapositions, mass imbalance and ground plane relationships instil the primal energy. These are not properties of a specific manifesto or philosophy, or Corbusier's concept of a machine for the living: they are the *intensive* properties of the architectural arrangement – relationships.

Associations

Shapes and their corresponding experiential associations meld into cognitive symbols, building blocks of perception. Some shapes or forms embody palpable energy, others imply its past presence or current potential, instability, impending nature or transience. The association becomes inherent to our *perception of the shape*, relating to our spatial experience and symbolic associations.

By association, particular shapes epitomise solidity, strength, structure or stability. Certain shapes infer motion. Others yield to gravity, or float with the wind or on water. To the technically inclined, specific shapes can negotiate isobars, isotherms or isoparms. Whether rectilinear, curvilinear, 2D, 3D, geometric, Platonic, pure, organic or fractal, they *may be implied by a mere representational fragment of their whole*.

Shapes influence massiveness, gravitational effect, buoyancy, sound and airflow. Shapes can inspire beauty. Shape and relationships reveal architecture; they *influence the experience* and can enhance its human value.

> The stones you have erected tell me so. You fix me to the place and my eyes regard it. They behold something which expresses a thought. A thought which reveals itself without word or sound, but solely by means of shapes which stand in a certain relationship to one another. These shapes are such that they are clearly revealed in light. The relationships between them have not necessarily any reference to what is practical or descriptive. They are a mathematical creation of your mind. They are the language of Architecture.
>
> Le Corbusier[46]

This language of architecture expressed by Le Corbusier is a visual language of shape and relationships – a visual language to which we respond cognitively and viscerally. Mass, void, light, shadow and borders help define it. The thoughts they express imply physicality. We perceive its energy.

Our visualisations are corporeally interactive; they can evoke emotional and physiological sensations.

The Human Response

Human response to a building's architecture emerges from instantaneous associations to visual configurations that include proximity and relationships. They can impart the perception of balance, placidness, vibrancy, discomfort or ill-health. Our responses to the simple visual components of a drawing demonstrate this tendency toward subconscious associations.

Visualisation is a total experiential involvement, a movie inside our heads with ever-changing scenes, cuts, close-ups and transitions through depth of field, subject and detail. This picture evolves in the perspective of real time and motion, as well as a sense of time and motion induced by eye movement, focus, head mobility and locomotion. Its objects convey physical and emotive characteristics. We frame their entirety or merely a part – configuration, orientation and perspective change. Some objects change shape: a bending arm, a blowing leaf. Others like a bicycle wheel skew shape with angle of view.

This *gestalt*, a world defined by perception of the moment based on accumulated experience, arises from the mind's interpretation of sensory input biased by our instinct and prior knowledge. Provoked by both visceral and cognitive responses, meaning emerges. We relate to architecture and the built environment in the same manner.

The mind searches for patterns, plucks order from chaos or anticipates chaos from order. Time, body movement, binocular vision, eye movement, focus, pressure, force, gravity, temperature, smell, taste, colour and luminance etcetera *map the experience of architecture*. Through a continuous processing loop that tests contemporaneous input patterns against stored knowledge, the brain establishes a united perception from the dynamic nature of our sensory inputs.

Once the mind defines or recognises an object or shape, we understand its physicality, its form and appearance in different orientations and views. We know how the object or shape must be oriented to provide the projection we see. If we see a wheel as an ellipse, we know that it must be obliquely oriented in our view. We understand the object as a circular wheel, not as one compressed to an ellipse. Simple line drawings can indicate form, orientation and distance for familiar objects[47]; as with the sketch in Figure 52.

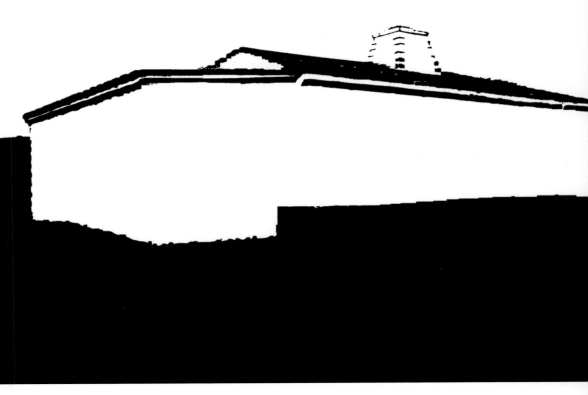

52. Rustic building outside of Longyearbyen,
Norway (graphic by author). © Bill Caplan

Despite that, simply summing the components is insufficient to experience the essence; the gestalt view coalesces into a coherent body with its own characteristics. As such, each of the *assembled parts acquires a new identity from the composite*. They are no longer a singular part like a metal rod; they are a component of the whole, the spoke of a wheel. The parts redefine with meaning. *Detail by itself does not define an experience* without a sense of the whole.

As we add new elements to an architectural design – altering a figure, shape, form or gesture – which addition significantly alters the energy vector by nature of its relationship to the proceeding one? Which element tips the balance of symmetry to asymmetry, the static to dynamic, becoming the tipping point? Which new element or series of elements crosses the boundary from *simplicity* to *complexity*? Whether conscious or subconscious, the tendency of these relationships to provoke human stimulation originates at an early stage of material propagation.

The way in which a point in space or an architectural moment can alter intensity through position or adjacency, or mere presence, demonstrates the forces inherent to relational interactions. By understanding our response, and the simple algorithms that energise architectural elements, we can inform the contextual value of new architecture.

The experiential nature of architecture relies on human perception, communicated in the energy of the arrangement of mass and void, shape, form, alignment and materiality. Herein lies the language of architecture, expressed by the architect. The experiential interfaces of architecture are *manmade*. As such, we have the opportunity to design them in an ecological and people-friendly manner. It only takes the desire to do so.

2 THE STRUGGLE FOR GREEN

1 *Sustainable Design is Human-centric*

▶ SUSTAINABLY GREEN –
Now and Forever

Our need to construct shelter as protection from the natural world has motivated building for millennia. Shelter building evolved from the utilisation and exploitation of natural resources for survival, to the creation of habitats designed for common benefit. Attending to human comfort and health evolved as well. In recent times, resource management and sustainment became acknowledged needs. Design consciousness progressed from individual survival and fulfilment to *green* living, from living green in the 'present' to *sustainably green* with an eye toward the future.

Although the use of passive design techniques to achieve interior environment comforts, such as utilising solar heat gain, natural light, natural ventilation, water collection and the thermal mass of earth and stone, has existed for millennia, the *imperative* for environmentally conscious design has yet to awaken the design/build industry on a large scale – despite its buzzwords infiltrating the lingua franca.

Recognition of the need to *conserve* and *protect* our natural resources is a relatively new concern. The first Earth Day on 22 April 1970 brought environmental consciousness to a worldwide audience, crystallising an environmental movement.

The year 1970 fostered a round of architectural experimentation that focused on how we live, what we produce and the viability of our eco-system. Michael

Reynolds' Earthship houses in New Mexico adapted age-old concepts of earth-based construction and site-based natural resources. Additionally, Reynolds saw the need to deal with the abundance of detritus. His philosophy called for harvesting natural resources and waste on the one hand, while conserving energy and resources on the other. The Earthships were earth sheltered, employing the landscape for natural protection and as a natural heat sink for temperature stabilisation as in Figure 53. The construction technique utilised earth-filled recycled tires for walls, their thermal mass to store solar heat for nightly re-radiation. Non-load-bearing walls were often studded with recycled containers to conserve matrix material, whether adobe or concrete. Rainwater and snowmelt were harvested as a water source (figures 54 and 55).

54. Earth-rammed recycled tire construction. © Bill Caplan

53. Earthship built into the landscape in New Mexico. © Bill Caplan

55. Recycled bottles and cans used as filler for non-load-bearing walls. © Bill Caplan

Paolo Soleri's Acrosanti community in the Arizona desert, also a product of the 1970s, was intended as a holistic experiment in human ecology. Soleri envisioned a community that could grow into a city of 5,000 inhabitants, a sustainable human habitat integrating architecture and ecology. Acrosanti was a laboratory for urban civilisation, a city for the future that addressed the depletion and pollution of the earth's natural resources and food supply – sustainable and green. These early experiments confirmed some of the principles of passive environmental design, but not much more.

Sustainability and green design are not new concepts, having been subjects of discussion and experimentation for nearly a half century. Sustainability is achieved partly through human behaviour and partly through building practice – conservation, recycling, reuse and intelligent disposal, and with methodologies such as passive design, new material development and technology. Nevertheless, the universal application of 'sustainable' and 'green' design in the built environment, and their systematic, effective implementation, remain far afield.

We build buildings for the benefit of people, and our desire to sustain a healthy ecosystem is human-centric as well. Our motivation to create a green built environment and to sustain our resources is to benefit people. Human benefit is the driving force behind human ecological design. To design buildings for humanity requires a green design that is *sustainable*.

Whether one uses 'green' or 'sustainable' is not important in itself; their definitions and usage are imprecise and they are often used interchangeably. 'Green' tends to be associated with living in a healthy environment in harmony with the natural environment, both in a building's interior and exterior. In building design and construction, green concerns the use of products and practices that are safe for human welfare and its environment, employing natural materials, site-based resources, renewable resources, avoiding unhealthy emissions and outgassing, and minimising waste. Although green design promotes environmental efficiency, conservation and protection, it primarily focuses on the present or near-term future, on one's own lifetime rather than on future generations. Sustainability address resiliency and longevity, the foundation for a green tomorrow.

Sustainability strives to address present needs without sacrificing humanity's needs in the future – to provide a green ecology now that also nourishes and preserves green resources for future generations. It promotes the use of green building materials for their positive effect on human welfare whilst, at the same time, factoring in the consequences of their broad environmental impact – *past, present and future.* The use of renewable, recyclable and recycled materials is part of the equation to lower the overall environmental footprint over their entire life cycle. This includes total energy usage and carbon footprint as well as emissions and pollutants. Sustainability requires a wide proactive umbrella to cover green design, one that protects and maintains long-term environmental health for broad social benefit, and necessitates *economic viability* for its long-term success. The World Commission on Environment and Development defined "sustainability" as "development that meets the needs of the present without compromising the ability of future generations to meet their own needs."[48]

▶ BUILDING DESIGN MAKES A DIFFERENCE – Whole Systems Thinking

From 1980 through 2012, the U.S. Energy Information Administration esti-mated that, on average, more than 80,000 commercial buildings per year were built in the United States. Over one million new buildings were built from 2000 to 2012,[49] all of which impact our quality of life and will impact future genera-tions as well. They interact with both the built and natural environment in one way or another. They utilise resources and have a physical and cognitive impact on their occupants and the community. Awakening to the importance of design to the population's current and future wellbeing, the U.S. government issued a memorandum on sustainable buildings in 2006. The federal government owned approximately 445,000 buildings at that time.[50]

The memorandum formally recognised that "these structures and their sites affect our natural environment, our economy, and the productivity and health of the workers and visitors that use these buildings", a nod to the unavoidable co-dependent relationships of people, what people build and the natural environ-ment – or in other words, to *human ecology.* Among other things, the memorandum encouraged "safe, healthy, and productive built environments" as well as "sustain-able environmental stewardship", a focus on *green* building practices to benefit a building's occupants while sustaining the future viability of the environment. Its purpose was to establish a set of guiding principles for sustainable building that is based on integrating all design parameters; systems thinking.

In order to achieve economic viability while addressing both aesthetic goals and a building's program, trade-offs are inevitable. Nonetheless, financed by the taxpayers, government building must not only serve the welfare of its occupants, but also the welfare of the greater community. All the people are *stakeholders*. This includes future generations.

The General Service Administration (GSA) is the U.S. government's landlord for non-military properties. Through its Public Buildings Service, the GSA is responsible for new building construction. Along with twenty other federal agencies and departments, the GSA signed this 'Memorandum of Understanding for Federal Leadership in High Performance and Sustainable Buildings'[51] in 2006.

The GSA distilled the following goals to promote the design of sustainable buildings, to improve building performance while creating healthy and productive environments:

- Optimise site potential
- Minimise non-renewable energy consumption
- Use environmentally preferable products
- Protect and conserve water
- Optimise operational and maintenance practices.[52]

Recognising that trade-offs are necessary in order to avoid "compromising the bottom line", the GSA philosophy seeks to achieve economically viable sustainability by reducing a building's impact to the environment, human health and comfort during *each phase* of the design process. This is to be accomplished by reducing consumption of non-renewable resources, minimising waste and creating healthy, productive environments through an "integrated, holistic approach", one that "positively impacts all phases of a building's life cycle, including design, construction, operation and decommissioning."[53]

Seeking a dialogue on the state of sustainable design's efficacy, as well as establishing benchmarks, the GSA sponsored a workshop for sustainable design "practitioners and thinkers" in 2005 with support from the Rockefeller Brothers Fund. With the theme 'Expanding Our Approach', the workshop "explored various ways of engaging in building and in the integrated design process that might lead to revolutionary, rather than evolutionary, gains..."[54]

Notably, 'Expanding Our Approach' embraced the discussion of social systems as well as natural systems within the matrix of sustainability's co-dependency with the built environment. Reaching a sustainable and equitable society was part of the conversation, as well as "place-based design, living systems analysis, and integral thinking."[55]

The forward-thinking participants understood that the GSA's desire to employ an integrated holistic approach anticipated more parameters than merely a building's mechanical systems and physical properties. The concept of 'whole' systems thinking also included the broad spectrum of "complex inter-relationships – natural systems, human social systems, and the motivating forces behind their actions – call it spirit, will, emotion, values, and so on." "Everything is connected – in the act of building design we are inextricably engaged in direct and indirect reciprocal influence in the immediate community (place) and the planetary systems we are part of."[56] The working group viewed sustainable design in the context of human ecology, to which it is inexorably entwined.

However, to date, the design/build industry tackles sustainable design purely in terms of a building's physical interface with our ecosystem, rather than the broader range of interfaces that include human experience and human-centric values. It is integrally tied to building codes, cash flow and profit in that quest for conservation of our natural resources, primarily energy and water, and the control of pollutants. A holistic approach that considers human behaviour is rare, one that integrates sustainable design with a building's experiential parameters and programmatic requirements is typically lacking.

According to the 2005 GSA workshop participants, "Most of us agree, however, that our current efforts fall far short of what is needed. Our current approaches are focused on reducing negative impacts."[57] "We are not routinely measuring the *effectiveness of our efforts[*] – we do not know if the performance of green buildings meets our expectations or the needs of the planet for a sustainable future". "'Doing less harm' is simply not enough."*[58]* These issues remain with us today, a decade later.

Sustainable design technique and technology have come a long way since 1970. We have had 40-plus years of scientific and technological innovation with which experiment, to learn what works and what does not. We have developed computer-based techniques to predict outcomes. The design/build industry in the USA has increased the promotion and implementation of sustainable design efforts substantially since the GSA's awakening in 2005. However, even with the aid of government suasion, regulation and subsidies, the *effectiveness of our efforts* is of significant concern – there persist many obstacles to achieving viable gains. As the science and technology of sustainable design is no longer new, this is surprising.

Green and sustainable design is achieved through the selection of building materials and the manner in which they are utilised to interface with the natural environment. Significant benefits accrue from utilising renewable, low-emission, recyclable materials on the one hand, and employing them for passive or active resource harvesting or generation on the other. Both their physical properties and their interfacial configuration are integral to the effective design and fabrication of the building envelope.

Advanced material technologies have added new capabilities to a building's skin. For example, glass and other cladding materials can separate heat from light, self-clean or air purify, generate electricity, store heat or ameliorate storm-water runoff. As need dictates, we can design an envelope's performative interfaces to function as receptors, collectors, reflectors, filters, insulators or depots to the large variety of environmental resources and encumbrances that engulf a site.

While architectural interfaces separate and distinguish environments, they can also bridge, interconnect or arbitrate their differences, often concurrent with the exchange of energy. Through this interfacial model, *the envelope functions as a mediating system*, separating environments that may or may not be in equilibrium and regulating spatial energy. The system orchestrates a course of action, an

---

[*]   Italic emphasis added by author.

algorithm that permits the envelope to absorb, block, transport, dissipate or store energy in order to mediate differentials or provide other benefits. *Environmental symbioses derive from such eco-friendly design techniques.*

Efficacy often comes down to educated selection and proper environmental site modelling. Most obstacles to the proper application of sustainable design can be easily overcome with technical assistance at an early stage of design development, educated selection and result-oriented design.

Unfortunately, even with a focus on minimising energy consumption, discard and pollution, tunnel vision often obfuscates the achievement of those design goals by ignoring the complete picture. Rather, they need to account for the past, present and future cost, waste and emissions – the *overall* efficacy.

2 Obstacles to Successful Execution

With the best of intentions, sustainable and human-centred designs often fail to achieve the intended goals. Many roadblocks and obstacles can thwart a successful outcome; the most fundamental derive from shortcomings in our educational system and a paucity of reliable performance information. Technical complexity and client-driven design can complicate matters as well.

Regardless of stylistic constraints or a design's theoretical underpinnings, it is a developer's desire for profitability, a homeowner's budget and taste, or an institution's desire for prestige that dictate the majority of designs built. *Clients choose the design.* Designs inspired by human ecological motivation are infrequent encounters.

Cost, code and construction efficiency drive design detail for most building, the ultimate resolution residing with the client – whether a developer, business, institution, government or homeowner. Profit drives the developer and business, budget drives the institution, government and homeowner, and architects must earn a living. In the pursuit of real-estate development and construction, maximising profit, expediency and marketing often trump human ecology and environmentally sustainable values. Marketing and the competitive incentive for saleability or uniqueness can lead to innovation for innovation's sake, or design as comfort food for the aesthetically inclined.

Although a matrix of contextual vectors typically provides the critical parameters for a fruitful design, a Petri culture to nurture the germination of effective architecture, attainment of such potential frequently dwindles during the design development process.

▶ "PR" VERSUS FACT –
Misinformation and Technical Complexity

Marketing Assertions and Unintelligible Specifications Often Guide Selection

Optimism, misinformed standards and misleading marketing obscure the proper assessment of new materials, sustainable design technologies and building methodologies. They often overlook the actual operating conditions, maintenance requirements and useful life, and fail to include the energy and pollution cost to mine and manufacture such products. The result is an illusion of substance rather than actual substantive gain, where suppliers profit at the expense of the consumer and the environment.

The increasing popularity and indiscriminate use of photovoltaic solar panels typifies the problem of uninformed application. Although not apparent in promotional materials, manufacturers' technical bulletins reveal that solar-panel power generation often degrades as much as 1% annually from ageing effects. Thus, they might function with as little as 90% productivity by the tenth year, generating 10% less electricity in that year. Likewise, they would produce 15% less in the fifteenth year and 20% less in the twentieth.

Promotional materials often lack other germane information as well. For example, the fact that electrical generating capacity decreases with increasing temperature and the effect this has on generation on hot summer days are rarely discussed, if at all. The same can be said regarding the reduction of energy generation due to shadows from a roof overhang, tree branch, vent or utility, not to mention accumulated dirt, soot, bird droppings, ice and snow. Reductions from soiled or shaded panels may be more significant than expected. Blocking the sun from reaching a *single* six-inch square (16cm square) crystalline PV solar cell of a panel of sixty cells can cease electrical generation in twenty of the sixty solar cells, one-third of the entire panel's surface.

Solar panels benefit the user and the environment when placed in the correct locations under appropriate conditions, but they do not have universal or persistent value. They have great value when deployed in solar farms, or in accessible rooftop or ground installations with unhindered solar exposure and easy access for maintenance or replacement. However, a significant number of home installations and installations on large-building facades are not environmentally sustainable or even financially viable.

Although engineers knowledgeable in the subtleties of photovoltaic systems can decipher their intricacies from a manufacturer's installation manual or specification sheets, architects, developers, homeowners, regulators, educators and the media lack comprehensible information. Many sales companies and installers are also vulnerable to this paucity of useful information, having to rely on oversimplified Internet-based applications to size and sell their systems, let alone determine their appropriateness for a given installation.

Similar issues exist with green roofs, solar screens, Passive House and Net Zero principles, super insulation, new materials and the like. Used appropriately, all provide significant environmental benefit, yet *they are frequently misapplied unknowingly*. Architects, developers, clients and most homeowners are not well versed in the intricacies of technical specifications and engineering details. They rely primarily on marketing materials and commercial reviews, sometimes falling victim to a fantasy unwittingly fostered by the trade and the architecture or building industries, often aided by equally misinformed government incentives and regulatory agencies.

The widespread misemployment of terms like 'green', 'sustainable', 'organic' and 'bio' as marketing ploys without substantive value, contributes to this misplaced optimism and valueless application. The same holds for the inclusion of sustainable devices such as solar panels, wind turbines or green roofs in projects or programs without justifiable gain.

Complexity is Hard to Maintain

Technically complex solutions to green design are another obstacle: they are subject to mechanical failure, electrical breakdown and chemical change over time – i.e. ageing. Their performance often depends upon a variety of external conditions, as in the solar-panel discussion above. Technical affordances can be a double-edged sword, offering energy generation or conservation, but with a high cost of manufacture, installation and maintenance. Manufacturing, installation and maintenance expend energy and add expense.

Many such systems have questionable value over time, some require expensive alterations in order to perform their function at start up, and some never justify their promise at all. Frequently, *performance failure is an unintended result of technical complexity.*

Kinetic architecture often falls into this category, as with the dynamic oculars on the Institute du Monde Arabe in Paris (1987), designed to be energy-saving sunscreens. The building's south-facing facade supports an interior brise-soleil composed of light-sensitive electro-mechanical diaphragms – their openings decrease in size with increasing sunlight. Progressively shading the interior as the sunlight increases along with its heat, they afford energy conservation, regulating the light and heat transmitted through the glass curtain wall (Figure 56).

56. Brise-soleil facade on a sunless rainy day, Institute du Monde Arabe, Paris, Jean Nouvel. © Bill Caplan

57. Constricted oculars in the left panel on an overcast day; all oculars should be wide open. © Bill Caplan

In addition to regulating interior light and temperature, and the facade's changing aesthetics, Jean Nouvel's bold design alters the *pattern* of filtered light as a function of the sun's azimuth and elevation angle and their influence on the apertures' size. Nouvel's ingenuity provides both a *performative and an experiential interface* with a modern reference to the Arabic mashrabiya.

Unfortunately, its complex mechanism is prone to failure. Many oculars freeze partially open or closed. Notice the closed central ocular in Figure 56 in the second column from the left, and the variety of closures in Figure 57.

58. The complex electro-mechanical
mechanism on the fenestration's interior side.
© Bill Caplan

Wear and failure of the system's motors and mechanisms mean that it requires
high maintenance, adding to the high monetary and energy cost of its manufacture and operation (Figure 58).

▶ WHEN LOOKS IGNORE FUNCTION –
The Dominant Role of Aesthetics

When aesthetics override function, context is abandoned. Obsession with aesthetic design often results in the disregard of a building's functionality, even when the overall theme projects an image of green design. We see this in corporate, civic and institutional buildings when the pursuit of an iconic image overtakes the tenets of the design goals.

The Bill and Melinda Gates Hall (Figure 59) at Cornell University (2014) was designed "using multiple strategies to create healthier environments, reduce energy consumption, and preserve natural resources".[59] Increased interior daylight and sustainability were two design goals.[60] Unfortunately, the facade's

59. Gates Hall, Cornell University, Ithaca, NY, Thom Mayne & Morphosis Architects, 2014. © Bill Caplan

aesthetic theme compromised the effectiveness of both. Although perforated steel solar shields shroud the glass curtain wall on three sides, to reduce the glare and heat gain, the sun's bright light, glare and heat penetrate the interior. The facade's high-tech design projects the appearance of green design, yet fails to deliver the benefits.

The architects conceived the solar shield arrangement to create "the illusion of movement through a series of rigid forms",[61] "a continuously dynamic and transformative surface".[62] However, the solar shields' reason for being – and performative efficacy – were lost in aesthetic translation. Disregarding sustainability, aesthetic design trumped function. Even though north-facing facades in the northern hemisphere do not require solar shielding, shields were appended to the building's north facade to continue the aesthetic theme. The *energy expended* to mine and manufacture their materials is sustainably negative; their life-cycle cost is wasteful of energy, a source of processing pollution and a significant financial burden to the client (Figure 60).

Although solar shields are appended where they are not needed, it is noteworthy that they are absent in some areas where they would benefit both the building's occupants and the client. No solar shields were provided for the exposed south and west facades of the top floor. And worse still, although the shield's design provides a futuristic high-tech look, sun and glare overpower the shields on the lower south floors, rendering the computer monitors inside difficult to read. They are not very effective. Occupants must pull down interior shades to shade the solar shades in order to use their computers (figures 61 and 62).

60. Solar shields on the north facade of Gates Hall, exterior and interior views. © Bill Caplan

61. South facade of Gates Hall and its interior, near noon on a November day.
© Bill Caplan

62. South-facing office on the top floor in Gates Hall around noon on a November day.
© Bill Caplan

The faculty requested natural daylight, not direct sun and glare. Uninterrupted glazing on a building openly exposed to the sun may be aesthetically pleasing, but it is fraught with sustainable design issues. Placing solar shields for their aesthetic effect completely misses the point. When aesthetics trump function and sustainability, purpose is sacrificed.

The bewildering array of materials, technologies and building methods available is itself an obstacle to successful execution. But in addition, misrepresentations of performance, uninformed application and technical roadblocks often interfere. Greater awareness is of paramount importance.

▶ TECHNOLOGY OVERLOAD – The Educational Dilemma

The challenge of maintaining education coursework current with the proliferation of new materials, technologies and building science constantly increases. As we learn more and more about sustainability and human-centric design, and how architecture interacts with human ecology, the philosophy and methodology of architectural design and construction change. A proliferation of new knowledge, new materials, new technologies and new building methods accompanies a proliferation of computer programs that can assist design, analysis and environmental simulation.

Many factions compete to shape the pedagogy and content of architecture schools, each with its own agenda. The National Architectural Accrediting Board (NAAB), the sole agency in the United States designated to accredit professional degree programs in architecture,[63] accredits more than 100 schools.[64] NAAB defines the *Conditions for Accreditation* and *Student Performance Criteria (SPC)*, revising them every five years. Interested organisations provide analyses and commentaries on the issues, offering their perspectives, sometimes with a competing agenda. These include the American Institute of Architects (AIA), the National Council of Architectural Registration Boards (NCARB) and the Association of Collegiate Schools of Architecture (ACSA).

However complex the NAAB's task of reviewing and reframing the criteria every five years, architecture schools face an even more daunting duty to revise their programs on a similar cycle. Administrations must allow the time for faculty to assimilate new requirements and the requisite knowledge base. Faculty must prepare new material, rewrite lectures, and alter studio and seminar syllabi without adversely affecting the overall program. The abundance of material already required in the architectural curriculum compounds the challenge. This represents a real burden to our educational institutions.

The pressure to incorporate new analytical and design tools, and new materials and technology, within the existing knowledge base emanates from the architecture and building industries. It enmeshes both NCARB's Intern Development Program and the Architect Registration Exams themselves. This requirement to expand the knowledge base and competency level competes directly with the demand for more licensed architects. Tight client budgets, short timelines and strained resources at existing architectural firms add another roadblock to the adoption of change.

For the 2009 and 2014 editions of *Student Performance Criteria*, the NAAB tried to address the proliferation of new tools, materials and technologies since adoption of the 2004 criteria, especially those related to sustainability, human welfare and safety. However, efforts to integrate this new knowledge and its potential benefits into existing building practice brought the competing priorities of the schools, the licence registration boards, the architectural firms and the developers into play. The different priorities of the 2009 and the 2014 editions evidence this discrepancy.

In 2004, sustainable design was included among the 34 Student Performance Criteria knowledge and skill categories, acknowledging the importance of environmental sustainability. It required students to demonstrate an *"Understanding of the principles of sustainability in making architecture and urban design decisions"*. By 2009, the collaborative process of integrated practice (IP) assisted by computer-aided building information modelling (BIM) was gaining importance. This too vied for broader inclusion in the SPCs, but faced mounting resistance to expanding requirements.

An Evolving Conditions and SPC Task Group 2008 draft opposed adding such courses simultaneously, to address curriculum "inadequacies" in sustainable design and integrated practice. They felt that the "'depleted yet overfull' curriculum could very easily get worse".[65] The abundance of new knowledge and skills required was overwhelming, then and equally so today.

Nevertheless, in 2009, not only did the NAAB upgrade its sustainability criteria to require an "*Ability* to design projects that optimise, conserve, or reuse natural and built resources", it related those skills to integrated practices. Merely "*understanding*" sustainable design was no longer sufficient: the NAAB now required competency.

Preparing its position for the next round of changes in 2014, the Association of Collegiate Schools of Architecture took the same stance as the SPC Task Group draft of 2008, asserting that "architecture curricula are full." "Additional expectations for technical training of graduates cannot be added without… reduction in other requirements or an increase in flexibility".[66]

The NAAB then **deleted** sustainability from the Student Performance Criteria in 2014. Its sole mention of sustainability refers to preparing "a review of the relevant building codes and standards, including relevant sustainability requirements" and assessing "their implications for the project".[67] The NAAB reduced the Student Performance Criteria for sustainability from having the *ability to optimise, conserve* or *reuse* natural resources, to being able to *review* relevant sustainability requirements and *assess their implications*. The "ability" to optimise, conserve or reuse was no longer one of the Student Performance Criteria.

The American Institute of Architects requires continuing education to sustain membership. In 2009, *sustainable design* education credits became mandatory. In 2013, that requirement was deleted:

> Recognizing that sustainable design practices have become a *mainstream design intention** in the architectural community, the Board of Directors has voted to allow the sustainable design education requirement to sunset at the end of calendar year 2012. AIA members will no longer need to complete the sustainable design requirement to fulfill their AIA continuing education.[68]

---

*   *Italic* emphasis added by author.

When mainstream design "*intention*" negates the need for knowledge, skills and continuing education, it is time to rethink the paradigm.

Architecture's relationships to human behaviour suffered a similar fate. The NAAB's 2004 *Student Performance Criteria* required students to understand the concepts that relate human behaviour to the physical environment. In 2009, the 'human behavior' *SPC* encompassed the triad of human ecology – the relationship of human behaviour to the "natural environment and the design of the built environment". Deleted in 2014, the Student Performance Criteria no longer include human behaviour.

It is true that "sustainable design practices" that respect low net energy consumption and the quality of the human ecosystem have become "mainstream design *intention*". However, our ability to turn those *intentions* into sustainable and eco-friendly built environments is far from reality.

New building products devised to enhance sustainability are entering the market at a rapid pace. Exploiting human behaviour as a design parameter has gained credence, surfacing in many graduate degree programs and research studies. Both *sustainability* and *human behaviour* are popular topics in the architectural trade press. Yet, over the last five years, the industry seems increasingly unable to digest this wealth of new knowledge and technology, tending to succumb to the *challenge of change* rather than capitalise on the opportunity it affords.

We already have the methodology and a surfeit of materials, products and technology; education is the critical catalyst for their productive application. It is the worst and least rational place to "sunset".

Sustainable design and human behaviour are central to the current dialogue concerning human health and ecosystem viability. Notwithstanding the difficulty of this challenge, the industry's ineffectiveness in tackling these problems more productively still perplexes. Perhaps to some, ecological thinking is an obstacle to design flexibility or profit. Others might see it as a more restrictive standard for licensing or government regulation. Regardless of the reasons, *education* presents a significant obstacle to productive design.

Abandonment of context, technical complexity, misinformation, educational dilemmas and the client's prerogative exemplify the many obstacles. Nevertheless, we can navigate these initial hurdles with an attention to ecological interrelationships, looking for opportunities for productive synergy. They can inspire innovative solutions for 'green design' that are consistent with the client's goals, effectuated by architectural creativity and engineering ingenuity.

3 HUMAN ECOLOGICAL DESIGN

① *The Concepts*

Human welfare – resource efficiency
– minimal environmental impact

▶ CONSIDERATIONS –
People and Environments, Energy and Matter

What is Human Ecological Design?

Human ecology scrutinises the interactions among people and their environments, both the built and natural environments. The terms 'people' and 'their environments' include human behaviour, interior and exterior sense of place, and the community. On a rudimentary level, human ecological interactions take place through interchanges of *energy* and *matter*, regardless of whether they are physical or cognitive exchanges.

Energy and matter provide the resources for everything we fashion and the means for its functionality. They sustain all life and the ecosystem's delicate balance, and issue the stimuli for human perception and action. Their properties influence both physical comfort and cognitive sensation. Energy and matter are the operative elements of human ecological design.

When we refer to the built environment, human ecological design is a process of conceiving, specifying and constructing buildings and infrastructures that *benefit human welfare* in a *resource efficient* manner with *minimal impact* to the natural environment. This includes the welfare of a building's occupants and users, as well as passersby and the broader community, and the local and global environments and their resources. Human ecological design's efficacy is measured in both current and future terms. It goes without saying that a successful outcome must effectuate the building's program and budget.

The principle underlying the human ecological design of the built environment is expressed in this book's opening premise, the truism that "*buildings are for people*". Any human alteration to the built environment should be designed for the benefit of people, which inherently includes the health and safety of the natural environment and the conservation of its resources. Building for people means *designing buildings with an eye towards 'green', towards 'sustainability' and towards experiential interactions* – designing buildings to suit their intent, while respecting the community and our ecosystem.

Human Ecological Design is a Non-zero-sum Game of Synergies

Erecting the built environment involves a game of competing forces: human activity and nature's ecosystem. Artefacts and the elements of nature are the game pieces. One player's gain might be another's loss, or might not be. The goals of *human ecological design* are to enable *life quality* and *sustainability*. This is a non-zero-sum game: success occurs when *all players gain*; smart strategies produce synergy.

Addressing the built environment, the purpose of human ecological design is to embed both human *and* environmental factors in the design process – not as individual objectives but as concomitant necessities. In other words, to develop each element of the design in harmony with human welfare *and* the natural environment. Energy-efficient features that are experientially undesirable defeat the goal. The same applies to experiential features that are environmentally unsustainable.

Human ecological design must be implemented on multiple scales to avoid unfavourable interventions by happenstance. Successful outcomes require a broad understanding of the design's inevitable impact on people and our ecosystem, the impact of its details and its entirety. Creating synergy requires *forethought*, proactive design with a view of both the nearby and bigger pictures. Human ecological design achieves outcomes by intention.

Multifunctional Thinking

Until the architecture interjects, there is only a site and the desire for a program. Prior to a new building's conception, the program is solely an *objective* to be satisfied. Site, defined by its terrain, the elements of nature, a community and an existing built environment, is a physical reality that predates the insertion of the architectural entity; it is more than an abstract lot on which to erect a building. The initial *site* restraints come first. Thoughtful design can harvest benefits from a site's ecosystem, infrastructure and community context.

The program objective and site characteristics influence the architecture; likewise, the architecture will influence the character and environment available to the program. There is a mutual dependency.

In building design, the exterior and interior are created to facilitate that program within the confines of a specific aesthetic and budget. A design must respect the site's physical properties, zoning, building codes and other legalities. Once built, it is an intervention that significantly influences its immediate environment – altering the site, creating new places and redefining the environment. These *interactions must be a part of one's consciousness* from the onset of design conception; they catalyse success or failure. Granted that architecture interfaces the entire locale, a responsibility to the local community's wellbeing and the ecosystem accompanies this intervention.

The key to forging simultaneous synergies among the program, the facility, the users, the community and the environment resides in considering the components of a building to be *multifunctional* interfaces, as being far more complex than interventions which merely separate space. Walls do designate and separate space, but their ability to influence the nature of these environments can render their capabilities even more significant. Architecture embodies both a physical envelope and an ecological opportunity – as materialisation and a mechanism. Employed as interfacial tools of architecture and engineering, the components of a building can be employed to benefit human ecology.

▶ SINGULARITIES –
Architecture Generates Change

We think of a building envelope as an enclosure, a shell. At a distance, shape and form become apparent; as we approach, material qualities and patterns appear. From the exterior, we see surfaces, yet upon entry enclosed space unfolds and the exterior disappears. We have progressed from distant snapshots to a continuous analogue experience.

Moving through an entrance or a door blocking the elements (wind, rain, cold or heat), or transitioning from night darkness into light, we focus forward, not on what we left behind – until we reverse the motion. We are not conscious of passing through an interface, through a portal that mediates two environments, yet that is precisely what happens. This common boundary between inside and out that frames the architecture by differentiating space, place and environment constitutes an interfacial system, a *singularity*.

Characterising the architectural envelope in operative terms in the contexts of the architect, engineer and human ecology, built architecture engages the world like the exogenous folds of post-structuralist philosopher Gilles Deleuze. The nature of its *interactions* – the transformations, inflections and convolutions – are "determined from without or by the surrounding environment."[69] Inflecting or convoluting matter, or the flow of energy, the architectural interface enables significant changes to a physical or sensible vector's direction or magnitude – embracing, reconfiguring or releasing its energy.

This philosophical perspective provides a means to construe the unique role of an interface as a 'singularity', having the ability to mediate exchange, or change the interactions of converging and diverging vector systems. This is exemplified in the complex exchange of heat energy through a building's windows and walls, between the interior and exterior environments, or the transmissions of light and images through glass in opposing directions.

In *Complexity and Contradiction in Architecture* (1977, 2002), Robert Venturi addresses the contrast often found between a building's inside and outside, the architectural "contradiction". He notes the design benefits achieved by freeing exterior design dependencies from the interior, the ability to accommodate or direct the aesthetic and function, as well as any space that emerges between unattached interior linings and the exterior wall.[70] Venturi explains that dramatic benefit occurs when form ceases to emerge solely from interior function – but rather as an interior and exterior convergence – producing an architectural event, an energetic point of change born from disparity.

> Designing from the outside in, as well as the inside out, creates necessary tensions, which help make architecture. Since the inside is different from the outside, the wall – the point of change – becomes an architectural event. Architecture occurs at the meeting of interior and exterior forces of use and space. These interior and environmental forces are both general and particular, generic and circumstantial. Architecture as the wall between the inside and the outside becomes the spatial record of this resolution and its drama.[71,72]

In their essay 'Symbiosis and Mimesis in the Built Environment' (2011), Luca Finocchiaro and Anne Grete Hestnes liken Venturi's way of separating exterior environment from functional program to the methodology of *sustainable design*, whereby "building form becomes a tool for the environmental control of comfort parameters, to mediate between the external–natural environment and the internal–artificial one." They explain that in the *sustainable design process*, form is reconciled more to the external environment than to internal program, revealed more in section than in plan.[73]

> While Le Corbusier focused on the architectural plan in his explorations of form, today's sustainable architects may focus on the architectural section instead, in order to achieve the objectives of breathing, symbiosis and the effective control of environmental phenomena. In the instance of sustainability, the section reveals the formal characteristics, dimensioning and composition needed for sustainable architecture.[74]

The section in this context relates to the architecture's *substance*, the arrangement and composition of interfacial materials, systems and spaces, and the opportunities of Venturi's "space in-between". A composite of singularities, the building envelope is more than a system of walls, roof and floor. It functions as a mechanism for change, a physical mediator of tensions between environments – the tensions Venturi sites between program and exterior. We understand them best in the sectional view, as suggested by Finocchiaro and Hestnes, which reveals the flow of energy, spatial perception and eco-compliant opportunity. When addressed, they energise architecture. To resolve them, the architectural design must emerge from, and respond to, the influence of competing environments.

The architecture, the common interface, must derive from and accommodate both systems, resolve them either in tension or in harmony, not as a cliff or a fracture. Cliffs and fractures are not productive interfaces; they create disparity. Such would be the case for architecture conceived without truthful context, merely serving as a container or boundary.

Singularities are states of uniqueness, of special qualities. They are energy and matter, moments for transformation, the bridges that negotiate a discontinuity or difference; functionally, they are mechanisms. Therein resides their uniqueness or special nature.

Like the contradictions often found between a building's inside and outside, a singularity is a contradiction, a mechanism of continuity that is not a continuation of its preceding format; exemplified by an inflection between curves or systems. *It is an interface.* In a mathematical and philosophical genesis, it is a point unto itself that exists within the system under observation. As an example, consider the *point of inflection* of a variable curve, the point at which concave transitions to convex (Figure 63). The inflection point does not follow either of the two curvatures it connects; the inflection point *is* the transition.

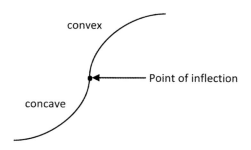

63. Inflected curve.

Deleuze referred to a point of inflection as the "ideal genetic element. ...the authentic atom, the elastic point."[75] In abstraction, this unique point exists within a system in the same manner as a point of location, or as a moment of duplicity generated by an algorithm with discordant outcomes, that emerge coherently from a single source. Herein lies the challenge in architecture, the in-between – *both generator and consequence.*

We may consider the point of inflection to be the consequence of two competing systems, their mediator. Alternatively, we can see it as *the seed that generates two subsequent systems.* In these examples, transitions occurred along a line, projecting the energy bound in emergence. Closely packing an infinite series of inflected lines can produce an *inflected surface* – a variable curve surface with a *line of inflection* as in Figure 64.

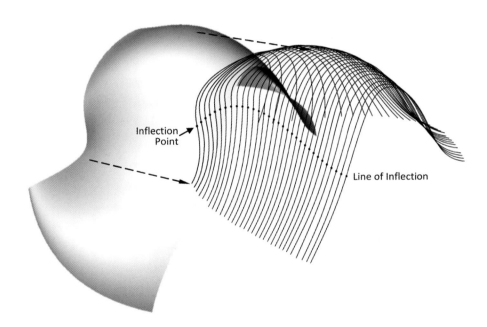

Inflection Point

Line of Inflection

64. An inflected surface depicted by a series of surface curves.

Greatly magnifying the view, we can imagine the atoms, points of inflection and their interstitial forces, energy fields, acting as physical members that transition energy or force. As such, singularities take on a physical meaning, a *matter and force field system.*

Peter Macapia inspired a deciphering of the building interface in terms of the singularity. In his studio, *Singularity*, at Pratt Institute Graduate School of Architecture and Urban Design in 2009, Macapia imbued the concept with physicality:

> A singularity is a knot, a maximum intensity, a transition from one state to another, a node of pressure – and when singularities are arrayed in a network, they produce astonishing flows of energy. Singularities are intensified nodes of material/energy relations which structure matter, space, events.[76]

Elaborating, he characterised singularity as "a physics notion", one that occurs during:

> the moment in which a system saturates itself with a behavior that forces a qualitative shift even though the basic matter hasn't changed.[77]

In this manner, we can model architecture as a congregation of singularities – material/energy relationships that structure matter, space and events. To Macapia, a singularity was not only an event and a world as expressed by Deleuze[78], but a physical system as well; like a grid compressing to become a continuous member, a beam. His model referred to a *system*, like one that produces a phase change. Think of water's phase change into ice or graphite's transition into a diamond. The singularity functions as both "verb and object". It is "not righteous engineering since it's aesthetic as well".[79] Macapia's elegant conception of singularity distils the emergence of architecture as an interface. This emergent aesthetic, the integration of a verb and an object, energises architecture.

In the architectural context, we can consider the interface of two distinct grids. As each grid is a functioning system, this is analogous to an exterior environment interfacing with an interior. Their surface or section of convergence is a singularity, its own system. In a physical sense, a singularity brings about this transition – an architectural event structuring matter and space as would a beam or continuous member in an interactive web (Figure 65).

From the engineering perspective, the constituents of an architectural envelope function like singularities as well. The barriers, filters, ports and structures are physical mechanisms of *environmental transition*. The environments they mediate

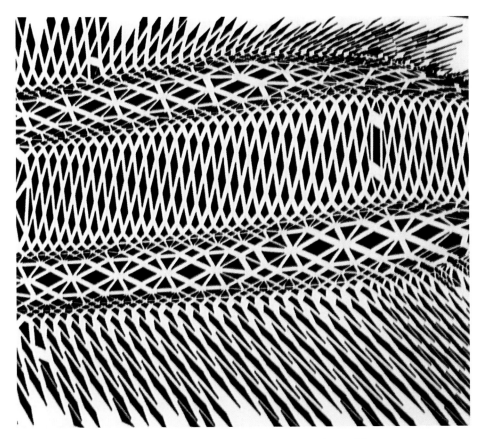

65a. Singularities emerge from converging grids.
65b. (Below) Forming a spatial structure. © Bill Caplan

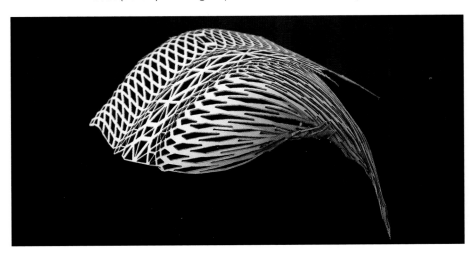

and differentiate influence their performance whether they are physical or experiential; they in turn influence the environments. In the architectural sense, two opposing systems bear upon the architectural singularity that mediates them, one pre-existing and the other newly formed.

This confluence of energy at the interface can lead to a moment that embodies changes or a chaotic rupture, each an architect's prerogative. In this context of an interface, the term 'singularity' means more than merely being unique, a singular design or creation. It occurs as a *departure from continuation*, a transition from the norm, ongoing, defined or regulated – a special instance. In other words, the architecture *mediates* the character and properties of the environments that it separates. In doing so, as *energy flows between these environments* in the form of heat, light, airflow, other things and people, a new environment emerges which alters the existing one.

In the context of a human ecological interface, built architecture emerges as something more than simple bricks and mortar. It materialises *integrally* with society and occupant, nature and program, energised with both activity and substance. *Built architecture embodies the powers of singularity, the powers of change.*

By directing its influence to inform the design, architecture can serve both the designated purpose and human ecology in general. Architecture is a material singularity – a physical transition – the composite of inflections between the entity, the program, the environment and our experience. Modelling this ideal provides a powerful means to envision the interactive capability of the architectural envelope and its design.

As a *mechanism*, the envelope is a tool of the engineer; as a *singularity*, although an abstraction to the mathematician, theoretician and philosopher, it provides a sensible palette for the architect.

Activating Architecture by Design

Sometimes, architecture emerges solely as a product of a program and budget, and sometimes from aesthetic aspiration alone or happenstance, offering little of value to the overall community or to the environment. To benefit human ecology, architecture must address all of its vectors – people, the built environment and the natural environment.

When design emanates from the convergence of these competing vectors, the architectural interface spawns both convergence and generation. As such, it is what Deleuze termed the "genetic element", "the elastic point."[80] The architectural DNA emerges from both external influences and the particularities of a program; it defines the plasticity of materialisation germinated by an architect's expression.

The *building envelope*, the architectural interface that separates the interior from the exterior – uniquely specific to a place, a program and time – is an interfacial composite of *surface* and *substance*. Creating space and providing shelter, these surfaces and substances modulate the flow of energy and the flow of people. This physical presence that affords the program is also a means for energy management and an aesthetic for community perception.

In essence, it exists as an architectural moment in its own world whilst being part of each world it separates. Surfaces and their substantive sections empower the transition; they are the mechanisms and singularities of human ecological design. Surface and substance activate architecture – they are multifunctional.

► AFFORDANCES – Surfaces Rule, Substances Regulate

The psychologist J.J. Gibson developed the concept that material things afford opportunities. In his book *The Ecological Approach to Visual Perception* (1986), Gibson models our terrestrial environment in terms of surfaces, substances and mediums,[81] eschewing the abstract world of bodies in space, geometric elements and coordinates.

The importance of surfaces, substances and mediums to humans is their *utility*, the qualities or actions they afford. To Gibson, the utility they afford suggested both verb- and noun-like qualities. Gibson thus coined the term 'affordance'. An affordance is an *enablement*, associated with a complementary *ability to be of use*. We can apply this concept to the surfaces and substances of a building, considering them in terms of their physical and actionable utility. They are affordances.

Our planet consists mainly of three states of matter – solid, liquid and gas. In Gibson's model, the interface between any two of these constitutes a *surface*.[82] Solid and semi-solid matter constitute *substances*; "a persisting substance with a closed or nearly closed surface" is an *object*[83]; and *mediums* are generally "insubstantial" and homogeneous. When any of these conditions provide utility, it is an affordance.

For example, Gibson explains that a *terrestrial surface* can be an affordance to humans for support, or for walking, kneeling, sitting, climbing, getting under or reclining. The *medium of air* is an affordance for breathing, seeing (transparency and light transmission), hearing (pressure wave transmission), smelling (chemical diffusion), ambient light (reflection), body movement (lack of resistance) or guided location (by sight, sound or smell from a substance at a distance). Terrestrial surfaces and air are affordances to humans because humans can utilise them. The affordance model provides a framework for multifunctional thinking, demonstrated by this broad range of opportunity made available by terrestrial surfaces and the medium of air.

Similarly, *architecture can afford many opportunities*; affordances comprise its *raison d'être*. In the context of human ecological design, architecture, having a broad spectrum of interfaces with the community at large and the natural environment, can afford more than just a platform for the client's program.

Affordances function by the agency of their interfacial qualities. *Surfaces* are interfaces that enable by means of their shape, texture, luminosity, materiality, or other physical properties. They can enclose, separate and define form and their benefits can be tangible or experiential. *Substances*, having surfaces, mass and volume can function as an interface too, they can affect an *exchange of energy over time* as would a process, determining the path, time it takes, magnitude and nature of an exchange. Whether surface or substance, affordances emerge from the energetic interaction of architectural moments, singularities. They too can be tangible or experiential, an expenditure, transmission or perception of *energy*.

When we perceive affordances, they offer their potential; when we utilise them, we realise their potential. Nonetheless, affordances exist whether or not we know they exist. Their value attaches to their use or their *potential* for use. For example, surrounded by walkable terrain, we can, or *know that we can*, translate to another location. Surrounded by water, we can swim or translate by boat, or see the affordance as a protective barrier. Such architectural interfaces are capable of influencing our activity and the condition of the immediate environment.

The persistent interfaces of architectural design affect the elements of human ecology whether or not we intend it, whether or not we perceive their existence – a fact to bear in mind.

Creatively addressing the elements of human ecology can afford a range of experiential, programmatic and environmentally beneficial opportunities; this is the operational basis of *human ecological design*. For example, the ramped exterior surfaces of the Oslo opera house in Figure 28 and the water feature in Figure 29 are *experiential* affordances, experiential opportunities for both visitors and people in the community.

Human shelter is a multifaceted affordance of essential importance, offering protection from nature's elements and other living things, safety within the community, physical comfort, mental health and wellbeing. However, the shelters we build also intrude on both the natural environment and the existing built environment. They interfere with the ecosystem, alter light and shadow, solar reception, thermal mass, airflow, water supply and runoff among many other factors. The act of building itself consumes significant energy and produces substantial waste. Beginning with raw material extraction and transportation, this continues through component fabrication, site preparation and construction. Opportunity is inherent in architectural and infrastructural design, but advantageous outcomes are not; they require fruitful implementation.

Thoughtful design and construction can reduce negative impacts, and even provide a basis for new ecosystems and community benefit. Architects and engineers have the ability to design structures with affordances that enhance both a program's effectiveness and the efficacy of its resources, thereby benefiting the occupants and the community as well as the client. *What architecture affords matters*, its interfaces are a key to the symbioses of human ecology, a *key to the beneficial exchange of human and environmental energy.*

Surface – Where the Action Is

The role of *surface* dominates the experiential nature of our physical universe, partly because surface is the most obvious and sensory constituent of physicality, but more importantly because *it is an object's interface* with its universe. As previously noted in Gibson's ecological model, an envelope's interactive properties occur at the surface, "*where* most of the action is".[84]

Aided by reflected or emitted light and the presence of shadows, we perceive the contours and textures of architecture by means of the surface, the tectonic and material qualities of its outer layer. When unobstructed by intervening partitions, we have visual access to the envelope's interior surfaces as well. The enclosure of space or the sculpture of its topography stems from the formation or manipulation of surface – whether continuous matter, a mesh or a conceptual boundary formed by an orchestration of objects.

Surface is also the first layer of *physical interaction*. Sound, reflected or emitted heat, smell and touch often enhance our initial impression. Our appraisal derives from phenomena reflected, emitted and absorbed at the surface, as well as by direct physical contact.

The surface is the outer limit of an envelope's skin, its face. Whether exterior or interior, a surface is both a cognitive and mechanical interface that exchanges and communicates energy. It mediates the movement of energy directly to or from the human sensory system, or in an exchange with the physical environment. One's initial impression of a building emerges from the perception of its surfaces' character and shape, which reveal sensory evidence of their physical and emotive qualities.

Cross-sections reveal the material makeup *and* the surface's boundaries; nevertheless *surfaces* are the interfacial feature, the building's outer and innermost layers, each of which influences its surroundings.

Surfaces are a key to human cognitive and emotional interaction; they facilitate architectural expression. In addition, they are the membranes through which environmental mediation occurs, providing the primary connectivity between the built environment and human ecological and social systems. Surface finish and colour easily demonstrate the significance of a surface's qualities. A glass pane's ability to transmit light or a crisp image greatly depends on its surface finish; a stone floor's surface is slippery when polished, safer for pedestrians when matte. Light-coloured surfaces reflect sunlight and heat; dark colours facilitate absorption. Substances interface through their surface.

The performance of the envelope's materiality works in concert with the properties of the substance's surfaces; together they form a mechanism for physical, visual and environmental change. Surface properties ultimately control the mechanism's potential to permit or cause actions, to assist a function. A surface is both a *catalyst* and a *permeable membrane* that selectively mediates the transfer and reactivity of energy and matter to and from the external and internal environments, as well as to the substances they bound. Although an envelope's material may appear as a solid or impenetrable barrier, it can absorb, react with and exchange energy in numerous forms, and be somewhat porous to moisture and gases. The surface itself is an interface, whose characteristics are key to the valuable role that a building envelope plays in human ecological design. The efficacy of surfaces is significant to human ecology.

Surfaces Are Real Yet Abstract

Although we can see, touch, interact with and walk on surfaces, their nature or reality is not obvious. They may incorporate physical properties that render them rigid, flexible, crushable or fluid, but their portrayal as an outer layer, coating or covering is an idealisation. Their interactive role can be obvious, yet the very *idea of a surface* is difficult to parse. Defining the fundamental elements of surface is a philosophical exercise, an intellectual puzzle.

The Notebooks of Leonardo da Vinci illuminate this mystery of surface.

> The contact of the liquid with the solid is a surface common to the liquid and the solid. Similarly the contact between a heavier and a lighter liquid is a surface common to them both. The surface does not form part of either – it is merely the common boundary. *Thus the surface of water does not form part of the water nor does it form part of the air...* What is it therefore that divides the air from the water? There must be a common boundary which is neither

air nor water but is without substance... A third body interposed between two bodies would prevent their contact and here water and air are in contact without interposition of anything between them. Therefore they are joined together and the air cannot be moved without the water nor the water raised without drawing it through the air. *Therefore a surface is the common boundary of two bodies, and it does not form part of either;* for if it did it would have divisible bulk. But since the surface is indivisible, nothingness separates these bodies the one from the other.[85]

Leonardo's surface is abstract, an indivisible boundary of nothingness that separates two substances, common to both yet not part of either one. We can perceive this surface optically, as in the case of water, but it does not seem that we can sail on Leonardo's surface.

Avrum Stroll's book *Surfaces* (1988) examines this dilemma.[86] Stroll interrogates the dichotomy between the obvious nature of an object's exterior (its surface) and the common boundary of two media (a surface), one physical, the other abstract. To the question "What are surfaces?" he suggests that they "form the upper or outer boundaries of embodiments."[87] We have direct access to the physical surface but perceive the abstraction. To characterise what he calls the *Leonardo Conception*, Stroll's discourse uses the term "interface" in its sense as a common boundary.[88] However, Stroll also explores the idea that an abstract surface can also be a physical part of an object, for example a billiard ball. Two billiard balls touch; each maintaining its own surface, yet the point of contact is a common boundary, both physical and abstract.[89]

In Gibson's ecological model, where a surface interfaces between any of the three states of matter – solid, liquid and gas – he distinguishes a *surface* from its underlying substance. A surface itself has physical properties like viscosity or elasticity, texture, composition and reflectance or absorbency. Gibson's surface has only one side, that "facing a source of illumination or a point of observation". It is an interface, an affordance, *where* "most of the action is" – what we touch, where vibration is transmitted, where vaporisation, diffusion and chemical reactions occur, and light is reflected or absorbed. A surface is substantial; a surface is textured.[90] One can sail on the surface of Gibson's water.

In 'Building Envelope as Surface' (*Aesthetics for Sustainable Architecture*, 2011), authors Sang Lee and Stefanie Holzheu merge Stroll's Leonardo Conception with Gibson's ecological model. Addressing the surfaces of architecture, this merger of concepts envisions both abstraction and physicality – *surface as a common interface*, an abstraction, and the *building envelope as a surface* in the ecological sense. Their surface is "An interface that mediates between the interior and the exterior, reflecting the relations and flows between the two" and a "membrane that at once separates and connects media and substance, ephemeral and permanent, dynamic and static".[91]

Lee and Holzheu liken this operative between the interior and exterior to the *fold* of Deleuze in the context of Gibson:

> Not unlike the Leonardo conception of surface, the fold offers a connection and an interface between matter and affectation. The fold articulates the connective tissue of two states – interior–exterior, object–environment, media–substance – as a process of folding and unfolding. Conceived in this sense, the building envelope is simultaneously connecting and separating, permeable and impervious, constant and fluctuating. A building envelope conceived as a *surface-fold* can be viewed as a condition where two states co-exist in a smooth and continuous relation, where the transition between the two is indivisible. What is crucial here is to establish the manifestation of the building envelope as surface, working from the conception of materiality in an *ecological sense.*[92]

Interestingly, their reference to Deleuze relates to activity, the "facade as an active agent"[93]. We can say the same for Gibson's surface, "where most of the action is."

Whether conceptualising surface in the abstract, as Leonardo's common boundary of water and air, or as a physical notion such as mediating their exchange of energy or reflecting visual light, *surface is an active participant* – common to two environments. This interface of activity and substance is the agent of architectural singularity, a catalyst in Macapia's system, a Deleuzian event.

Surface is the interfacial tissue of the building envelope, communicating environmental energy to the substance it bounds, and the envelope's energy to the environment it faces and the people in its sphere.

A building's exterior surfaces establish its boundaries; their arrangement and composition put forth the design. In conjunction with the interior surfaces, they instil an identity, a sense of place and functionality that governs the parameters that are easily accessible to the program and the ecological interfaces. The envelope's surfaces project an aesthetic or style and frame the spatial planning and circulation. The manner in which architects and engineers design these surfaces is crucial to successful architecture. The manner in which they design an envelope's cross-sectional substance is of major importance as well.

Surfaces Need Substance

No interaction occurs without surface; however, without substance, surface is an abstraction.

Surfaces need *substance* to process and regulate the admission of natural light and view, the exchange of thermal energy and numerous other interactions. Whatever a building's surface coverage in elevation or plan, it is the arrangement of the material cross-section, its substance, that enables performative execution. Both the building envelope and the entire built environment are permeable membranes that interface with daily life and the local environment, but their level of activity relies on the properties of their substance.

Together, surfaces and their material substance embody the building envelope. Surfaces activate the qualities; they are facilitated by the cross-sectional composition, the substance (Figure 66).

Functioning both individually and together as a system, surface and substance afford significant design and performance flexibility from a large matrix of materials, finishes and mechanisms. This provides a broad range of aesthetic and performative opportunities. By distinguishing the individual characteristics of each segment of the composite, we can better understand how the envelope functions as an *interfacial system*. The significance of each component, surface and/or substance emerges in terms of its interactive functional capability.

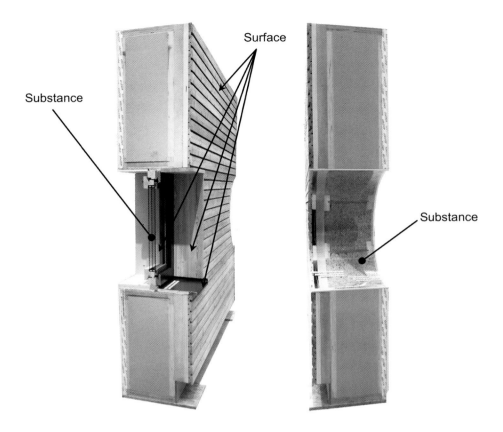

66. Cross-sectional substance and surface: skin, structure, insulation – barriers and ports. PassivHaus wall by Lumar. 2014 Architecture Biennale, Venice, Italy.
© Bill Caplan

Each system sector contains a surface that relates to one or more material substances or to a void, and the sectors work together in some fashion as a mechanism or enablement. Every medium, substance or environment in contact with the envelope contains energy, and takes part in the transfer energy when not in equilibrium. Each surface sector interacts with energy whether or not intended. *Never energy inert*, the envelope continuously mediates the exchanges of environmental and perceptual phenomena at various scales.

Working together, they are able to serve many functions, notably environmental control and energy management. Surface sectors can deflect or reroute the elements of nature as well as vent the interior environment. They can also play a major role in energy transfer, conservation or production through absorption, emission, transmission or retention and, in some cases, generation. This includes the exchange of energy both with the environment and with people, whether physically or cognitively induced.

The architecture of a building envelope can incorporate numerous interconnected surface/substance sectors designed to function in multiple physical, operative and sensible manifestations. In many ways, this ties Macapia's knot. Artistically and purposefully, the interlacing of sectors is analogous to a *seam*, conceptualised as something more than an expedient by Gottfried Semper, an architect and theorist of architecture and style. In *Style in the Technical and Tectonic Arts; or, Practical Aesthetics* (1860), Semper addresses the importance of the seam itself as a unifying connector to a common end.

> The seam is an expedient that was invented to join pieces of a homogeneous nature – namely, surfaces – into a whole. Originally used in clothing and coverings, it has through an *ancient association of ideas* and even through *linguistic usage* become the universal analogy and symbol for any *joining of originally discrete surfaces* in a tight connection. A most important and prime axiom for artistic practice... *the principle of making virtue out of necessity*. It teaches us that anything that is and must be patchwork... should not be made to appear otherwise. If something is originally separate we should characterise it not as *one* and *undivided* but, by deliberately stressing how the parts are connected and interlaced toward namely, a common end, all the more eloquently as coordinated and unified.[94]

Semper's seam is an entity in itself, not a homogenised meld interlacing the surface of surfaces. In a broad sense, interlacing qualities of the places it ties together, a building envelope signifies architecture's seam – a seam of human ecology.

The primary operators of human ecological design are the envelope's **surface** *and* **substance***. The creative selection and utilisation of surface and substance can accomplish incredible people-friendly and environment-friendly architecture. They are the most significant components of green design and sustainable operation.*

2 The Parameters of Human Ecology

Life is contextual.
Contexts have parameters.

▶ RELATIONSHIPS – Parametric Design

Since the advent of architecture, creating shelter has entailed a parametric process of design. We have always constructed buildings to serve a purpose, to meet specific needs and to respond to physical realities – these are the parameters. Whether they address the relationships between use and volumetric constraints, or building codes, zoning regulations, a palette of materials or other contexts, those *relationships regulate the construct.* They relate to its *raison d'être,* the conditions it must contend with and the client's dictates. Parametric design attaches a design characteristic to specific conditions. This applies at all scales, from a small detail to the tectonics of shape and form.

Parametric design does not require a computer. It is inherent in heuristic rules of thumb, such as Vitruvius' use of eastern light for bedrooms, western light for winter baths, and northern light for picture galleries.[95]

The process considers the physical, performative and experiential interrelationships between project components and vectors of the global environment. Each parameter relates to others, influencing the flow of energy and resources, affecting our sensory system, the environment and perhaps the budget.

We see this type of interconnected forethought in Lawrence Halprin's master plan for the Sea Ranch community in northern California in the early 1960s. It was central to his methodology for developing human environmental designs, expressed in *The RSVP Cycles* in 1969[96]. Wind, erosion, soil, vegetation, forest condition, drainage, sun, view, ocean, ground elevations, future community, open space, common space, living space, access, income levels and marketability are some of the parameters comingled in Halprin's process of emergent design.

The Sea Ranch plan envisioned a community of buildings designed to link with nature, commonly sharing large areas of the site's coastline (Figure 67). Halprin planned for a cluster of houses around a hedgerow linked in a "village-like quality". Following the line of the hedges, the rooflines would "control" the wind, creating a protected garden behind each house.[97] Human habitation, natural surroundings, light, views and the strong winds were the contextual vectors, the design parameters (figures 68 and 69).

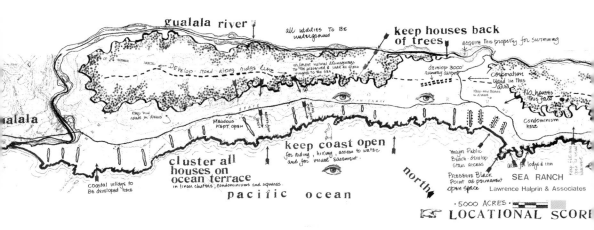

67. Sea Ranch plan for action, by Lawrence Halprin,[98] provided by The Architectural Archives, University of Pennsylvania by the gift of Lawrence Halprin.

68. Wind vector calm zone sketch by Lawrence Halprin[99] provided by The Architectural Archives, University of Pennsylvania by the gift of Lawrence Halprin.

69. Sea Ranch house, designed to create a wind vector calm zone. © Bill Caplan

In addition to the cluster housing, the plan called for multi-unit condominiums. Moore, Lyndon, Turnball and Whitaker designed the only one actually built. Although significantly larger in scale than the houses, the condominium's design was driven by the same parametric vectors. Parameters were chosen to benefit from the sun's radient heat, to enable views, respect the wind and to incorporate local barn-like vernacular references (Figure 70).

Unfortunately, as the project expanded, some of the parametric constraints were abandoned – the developers lost track of Halprin's intent.

70. Condominium 1, Sea Ranch, 50 years later, Moore, Lyndon, Turnball and Whitaker. © Bill Caplan

Computer Assisted Design

A keen interest in parametric methodology prevailed in the late 1950s and early 1960s, to apply parametric mathematics to architectural design and urban planning. Founded in 1957, Luigi Moretti's *Istituto per la Ricerca Matematica e Operativa applicata all'Urbanistica* focused on such research. Some of his *Architettura Parametrica* models were displayed in the Exhibition of Parametric Architecture and of Mathematical and Operational Research in Town-planning at the twelfth Triennial Exhibition in Milan in 1960. Moretti designed the Watergate Complex in Washington, DC (1965), purportedly one of the first buildings to utilise computer-aided design for construction.

Our ability to integrate site, environmental and human parameters with the design process has increased significantly since that time. Computer-based parametric design tools became available commercially in the early 1980s, becoming widely available in the first decade of 2000.

Avion Marcel Dassault in France developed 3D design software for the in-house design of their jet fighter aircraft in 1977. The software was available commercially as CATIA® in 1981. AutoCAD® was released in 1982. In 1991, Frank Gehry used CATIA® to design the Guggenheim Museum in Bilbao. Since 2004, Generative Components®, Maya®, Grasshopper®, Revit® and many other programs have brought parametric design capabilities to the broad community of architects, engineers, designers, academics and researchers.

With this software, design can be controlled not only by dimensions, but also by other parameters such as site features, material properties, solar movement, weather patterns and a multitude of designer-specified relationships. Maya®, developed for movie animators to create virtual environments, includes a means to simulate gravity, fluid effects and flexible materials under dynamic conditions. Revit®, created specifically for the architectural design and building construction industries, enables building design and modelling with pre-programmed three-dimensional building components. Many programs incorporate simulation of the sun's movement, casting light and shadows. By 2009, even new releases of AutoCAD® incorporated parametric functions.

Frank Gehry's use of CATIA® to design the Guggenheim Bilbao twenty-five years ago stimulated great interest in *parametric form generation*. Although the potential for *parametric design* integrating architecture and the environment was widely discussed, metaphorical aesthetic flourishes and building information modelling (BIM) remain its principal use. Employment for environmental design and human synergies has made little progress.

Parametric design and modelling enables architects and engineers to assign numerous programmatic, regulatory, material, structural, environmental, social, cultural and budgetary relationships to influence design maturation. Selectively applied, these parameters can assist in the conception of form. Computer-rationalised relationships can finesse the design of individual facade or roof panels in response to their surrounding microclimates; maximising performance as influenced by adjacent buildings, trees, climatic swirls and the like. This genre of analysis and design control enables a broad spectrum of new opportunities, from design generation, to its testing, verification and detailing.

Parametric software turns a designer's mouse into a sculptor's tool, enabling the visualisation and creation of fantabulous forms. At the same time, it can integrate multiple parameters from the site and locale with the client's goal and human behaviour, linking all of them to the designs conceived by the architect. *Parametric design can link performance to expression.*

► PARAMETERS – Vectors from N, S, E, W; from Above, Below and Within

Structures in our built environment interface with their communities of people, their physical surroundings and natural phenomena. This constitutes an ecosystem in which all parts are interdependent. Each ecosystem element has a region of activity, within which its attributes comingle with attributes of the other elements in its sphere. The attributes of a building, its physical surroundings and the natural phenomena, and the attributes of the users and the community, are the *parameters* of human ecology. Together they comprise the *context* in which a building exists, in which we evaluate its performance. Context creates parameters.

We experience a building in the contexts of its physicality, its program and its surroundings. This includes tangible and intangible parameters tempered by one's personal perspective as the occupant, user, passerby or member of the community at large. We evaluate its efficacy in the context of its goals, perhaps its operating or building cost, its energy consumption or long-term sustainability, its emissions or runoff, or its influence on other buildings, sites or the natural environment. In every case, a parametric relationship exists among salient attributes of the goals and contextual realities. There are many contextual spheres to juggle – all overlap.

The parameters that determine a building's performance are mutually interdependent. They influence each other's outcome and characteristics. The endeavour to catalyse site-based designs sensitive to the interplay of human instinct, response and wellbeing relies on *a pre-design consciousness* of the contexts and their parameters. Together they form a broad framework of conditions that define the fundamental aspects of human experience and environmental reality. They categorise a network of site intervention potentials that can interface beneficially with its surroundings.

The relevance of each specific parameter relates to the dictates of the client's program in conjunction with the contexts of the users, the community and the local built and natural environments. Together with the client's program, they form the parametric matrix in which the new entity will exist. Once built, architecture's influence enmeshes human ecology, altering the pre-existing. Contextual synergy is paramount to the realisation of a human ecological design. With foresight and proactive design, it can foster human and ecological synergies.

Proactive parametric design is not a new idea: in the case of Vitruvius' rules of thumb for geographical light, it is evident in his attention to aesthetic principles, culture, climate and a site's environmental phenomena such as wind direction.

> ...laying out of streets and alleys with regard to climatic conditions. They will be properly laid out if foresight is employed to exclude the winds from the alleys.[100]

Sensitivity to context, the key to human ecological design, anchors sound interrelationships and the condition sets to which they respond. The client, program and user, as well as the community, the built environment and the natural environment, are ineluctable elements of a building's pre- and post-development context. Built architecture's success relies on responding to a parametric matrix that includes its programmatic requirements and their contextual realties, not on its artistic nature and spatial allocation alone.

Once a building arises, its interactions with the human and ecological parameters of its locale do not cease. Rather, *they persist – whether in synergy or in opposition.* Contextual engagement must be a guiding tenet of the design process to optimise a building's viability.

Every thought, physicality and experience takes place with regard to some context – even if that context is a void or absence. The circumstances and conditions that endow meaning establish its relevancy. They make available a matrix of parameters.

The Parameters of Human Ecology Are Vectorial

Each parameter of a client's program, a user's experience or a community's interaction is a *vector*. It has an origin, a magnitude and a direction of influence. The same holds true for each parameter of the natural environment and the built environment. Likewise, each parameter of a newly built entity will bear vectorially on its surroundings, the community and its occupants. Buildings themselves invoke contextual vectors that alter the nature of the surroundings. Each interaction influences the way we live. Each component of context is a potential design parameter. Some parameters bear on the built architecture, while some parameters of the built architecture bear on people and the built and natural environments.

The impact of each vector will relate to its nature, active direction, magnitude and its relevance to the object under its influence. Environmental interactions with the architecture and its locale are physical; corporeal interactions with people are sensorial. The effects are manifest in the performative and experiential aspects of the architecture relating to the occupants, passersby and the environment. Though some of the vectors engage architecture's material and performative characteristics while others engage its sensible values, *they all ultimately affect the human experience.*

The contextual roots of a building and its architecture are fundamental to its synergy with human ecology. *Context awareness affords proactive design.* Respecting or exploiting tangible and sensible properties can enhance architecture's ecological value. Identifying these parameters and their course of action is the first step of this *proactive* methodology.

The design of a building's surfaces and substance is most beneficial when it creatively addresses a parametric matrix of relevant contextual vectors.

3 *Performative Expression*

A building envelope expresses architecture's aesthetic and character, often mingling tectonic shape, materiality and the arrangement of mass with decoration and ornamentation. Artistic elements of the built environment transform our visual experience, whether conveyed by a building's form or by what we deem to be decorative.

For some theoreticians, critics and students of architecture, decoration is appropriate only when intrinsic to the architecture's DNA, as structure or skin or fenestration; otherwise, it constitutes unnecessary embellishment. To others, embellishments enrich style. Whether or not decoration and ornamentation are deemed worthy by the viewer, or by discourse or dogma, they play a significant role in human ecological design. Aside from their visual value, decoration and ornamentation physically interface the environment in the same manner as other elements of a building's construction. In concert with their sensible properties, a building's expressive elements can provide performative interactions. *Expression is not only visual; it can be experiential and functional as well.*

▶ TROPE AND STYLE –
Symbol or Substance

It is difficult to discuss the aesthetic qualities of architecture without alluding to stylistic categorisations. The mere mention of specific architectural gestures, ornamental embellishments or decoration, let alone architectural genres such as churches and houses, summons the notion of *style*. For many it is the first thought or word associated with architecture, the instantaneous recall of form, character and detail, and the manner of their expression. Categorisation and classification are important tools that assist communication and memorialisation; with them, we develop the language, nomenclature, syntax and rule sets that constitute a 'style', permutations of a building's structural arrangement, shape, mass, materiality and detail.

One's individual response to a building will emerge from a gamut of stimuli and triggers pertaining to historical associations and prior experiences, artisanship and decoration, and visceral reactions to mass, form and energy value. We tend to have personal preferences for specific styles or their attributes, favouring some, perhaps disliking others. Response to style is personal, tied to evolving societal, cultural, experiential and cognitive inputs that forge and change taste.

Architects and designers frequently conceive a stylistic trope based on a metaphoric reference to seed the creative process, its symbolism limited only by one's imagination. A language of form and syntax expresses the context and pattern development, evoking the theme for experiential stimulation. Architectural tropes commonly reference historical precedents such as the ubiquitous Greek temple and other classical styles. In one form or another, classical architecture has influenced design through the early twentieth century and remains a trope that influences government and institutional architecture as well as suburban subdivisions, 'McMansions'* and the like. The Modern movement sparked a significant change in architectural thinking, spawning the International Style and subsequent permutations in the latter half of the twentieth century.

Curiously, classical architecture and its derivatives have remained popular for 2,500 years, often as a touchstone for beauty, stature or soundness. Nevertheless, new styles will continuously emerge and tastes will change. Amalgams of style will proliferate, merging old with old as well as old with new; some might emerge from 'green' design or visions of the future, while others may lack any reference at all.

---

* An unflattering term used to describe a large house oversized for its lot or setting, often with a mixture of ill-matched or ill-proportioned stylistic references.

Nevertheless, typology by itself does not spawn beauty, nor does it generate stimulation or synergism. Likes, dislikes and ambivalences emerge from one's experience and frame of focus, regardless of the categorising style. Efficacies and synergy with the environment derive from performative interfaces residing in the execution of a designer's expression, not in its typology. *Human ecological design is not at all about style.*

The use of a *trope* as a creative design tool in architecture pedagogy is widely encouraged. Its human value, however, is not in its ability to seed a theme, but in its physical, operative and sensible execution.

Feel the Trope

Eero Saarinen's TWA Terminal 5 (1962) at JFK Airport in New York exemplified *experiential architecture.* Saarinen enhanced the language of modern architecture, enriching its potential through tropes realised in flowing organic form. One's experience commenced under the terminal's arrival canopy, engulfing the traveller. It enticed you into a futuristic fantasy from vehicle to aircraft (Figure 71).

From the intertwining paths and sweeping curves of the vaulted lobby, to the remote boarding satellites accessed through arched tunnels, the architecture conveyed the dynamism of air travel. The design provided more than an aesthetic or a sense of place: Terminal 5 was an experience. Saarinen described his trope as "uplift", an "upward soaring quality of line" to create "a place of movement and of transition", expressing the "drama and specialness and excitement of travel"[101] (figures 72, 73 and 74).

Commissioned in 1955, notably though a *pre*-computer design, TWA Terminal 5 influenced the works of Frank Gehry, Santiago Calatrava, Zaha Hadid and many other sculpturally expressive architects of the twenty-first century.

71. Arriving at TWA Terminal 5, JFK Airport, NYC,
Eero Saarinen, opened in 1962. © Bill Caplan

72. Uplift, TWA Terminal 5, JFK Airport, NYC.
© Bill Caplan

73. Architectural movement and transition, TWA Terminal 5, JFK Airport, NYC. © Bill Caplan

▶

74. Upward-soaring vaults and bands of light, TWA Terminal 5, JFK Airport, NYC. © Bill Caplan

159

The Visceral

The Jewish Museum Berlin, previously mentioned, expresses experiential tropes of another kind through a matrix of symbols and metaphors. Libeskind's architecture evokes emotions, connecting the contexts of a place to its history. Although some of its symbolism is discernible only with guidance, most of Libeskind's tropes provoke a visceral experiential response.

The building's zigzag ground plan symbolises a deconstructed Star of David. However, due to its scale, the deconstructed star is intelligible only in a drawing or an aerial view. The same holds true for other lines drawing imaginary vectors to pre-war homes of Jewish cultural figures. Yet, there are numerous tropes of a sensible nature, viscerally disconcerting; they augment the emotional value of the museum's displays. The disorienting zigzag path through the museum, its skewed floors, irregular and asymmetric incised fenestration, zones with sealed access, voids and lack of location references induce a sense of loss of control, fracture, isolation and imprisonment (figures 31, 75, 76 and 77).

75. Jewish Museum Berlin, Studio Daniel Libeskind. © Bill Caplan

76. Irregular incised windows in stairwell, Jewish Museum Berlin. © Bill Caplan

77. Void space, Jewish Museum Berlin. © Bill Caplan

The Fanciful

Computer-assisted parametric design opened new horizons in the 3D visualisation and manipulation of metaphoric form, enabling the design and fabrication of double curvatures. Fanciful references became definable and dimensional. We see this in Frank Gehry's Guggenheim Museum in Bilbao of 1997 (figures 26 and 27), the Walt Disney Concert Hall in Los Angeles of 2003 (Figure 78), the IAC building in New York of 2007 (figures 16 and 17) and the Fondation Louis Vuitton of Paris in 2014. All of these buildings express his fascination with flow and curvatures, the dynamics of fish, sails and boats, tropes that *visually* define Gehry's architecture.

78. Sails: Walt Disney Concert Hall, Los Angeles, Frank Gehry. © Bill Caplan

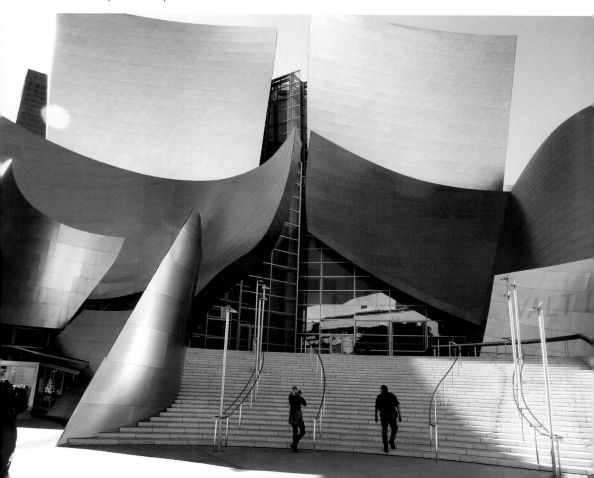

79. Ribbons: Hotel Marqués de Riscal, Elciego, Spain, Frank Gehry. © Bill Caplan

The Disney Concert Hall's form, Gehry's first design of this genre, commenced in 1988, predates the Guggenheim Bilbao despite having been completed six years later. The sculptural fantasy of its exterior carries through to the interior. His later works rarely bring such flourishes to the internal architecture; experiential tropes wane on the inside.

The flowing ribbons of Gehry's Hotel Marqués de Riscal in Elciego, Spain (2006) form a grand stylistic statement literally applied (Figure 79). Its flamboyant style is the Gehry brand – sculptural art. It is a visual artistic gesture, but little else.

Saarinen's influence on Gehry's artistic style is apparent. However, although Saarinen envisioned architecture as fine art, his aspirations were broader than art alone. He advocated that a "building cannot be *placed* on a site, but that a building grows from its site".[102] He valued the overall human experience, the exterior environs to the program, "uniting the whole, because the *total environment is more important than the single building*".[103]

Unfortunately, clients and developers frequently ignore the 'total environment' and so do parametric form-finders. Nurturing an aesthetic vision to be harmonious with the total environment, as well as the contextual parameters of the client, the program and its users, is not an easy task. Architectural design is complex. Nevertheless, when a trope communicates through substance rather than window dressing, when its matrix of parameters addresses human experience and environmental interaction, it can be highly effective. Identifying a broad spectrum of *contextual parameters* can catalyse human ecological design, resulting in something more than an artful expression.

▶ SYMBOLISM – Image versus Essence

Contextual interfacing is a powerful tool for architects and designers. It provides a means to achieve relevant and effective interactions with the salient characteristics inherent to a site and its infrastructure – physical phenomena, natural phenomena, culture and community. When architectural design neglects these considerations, the resulting architecture loses its bearing, and functions merely as a container for the program.

Many factors inspire the creative process and influence its outcome. Whether inspiration derives directly from the designer or in response to the market or a program, the creative process itself is intensely personal. The context of *self* is inherent to human creativity, nested within the creator.

Attuning oneself to a broad spectrum of contexts, such as those already related, is not necessarily inherent to the creative process or inevitably a part of creative fertilisation. When contextual sensitivity is not designer-driven, its parameters will have minimal influence, their *value often lost between concept and execution.*

Some building designs evolve under the *guise* of a trope or synergistic claim that is merely a metaphor for design, a device that is discarded once a concept germinates so as not to encumber project development. Although an effective methodology to initiate design, or to create a convenient rule set for its derivation, the trope itself provides little meaningful expression or legibility.

Even when such tropes are a key to a design discourse, without a well-founded contextual execution they are unlikely to fulfil their intent. Their references often exist in obscure ways, adding little to the outcome, perhaps in name only. The symbolic or metaphorical value of a matrix-defined trope is often lost in material translation. The figurative aspects might remain, but only as a cliché for PR material and client presentations. Evaluating a new work of architecture, professional critics often overlook a lack of meaningful carry-through, taking for granted the purported influences. Unfortunately, in such cases, the *critiques* lack the appropriate criticism.

Empty Symbolism Abandons Context

When symbolic references are flawed, even the cliché misses the mark. A well-known glassworks markets a line of crystal barware known as the "street collection". They advertise that "the hand-cut grid pattern of STREET suggests Manhattan's famous street network"[104] (Figure 80). As Manhattan's street grid is primarily rectangular not square, the reference is lost in translation.

80. "Street" collection hand-cut crystal glassware. © Bill Caplan

167

Similarly, the street-grid tropes configuring Peter Eisenman's unfinished City of Culture of Galicia (1999–2014) were also lost in translation. Unlike Gehry's accessible tropes, Eisenman's symbolisms offer little perceptible correlation to their metaphors. Eisenman applied four tropes as parametric inputs to drive the design matrix: (1) Santiago de Compostela's medieval street plan, (2) a scallop shell's footprint to define the outer boundaries, a symbol of the Camino de Santiago Pilgrimage, (3) a Cartesian grid to represent the modern city's street plan, and (4) the site's hilltop topography. Aided by algorithmic software, the designers finessed building forms from the topography as defined by the two grids and the

81. Concept model (below) and partially completed buildings (right), City of Culture of Galicia, Santiago de Compostela, Spain, Peter Eisenman. © Bill Caplan

scallop outline. Parameters from the four tropes formed a matrix to guide form generation and its surface decoration. Although the surreal architectural land-scape continuum has an extraordinary sense of place unique unto itself, none of it speaks to the medieval or modern city, its street grids, the pilgrimage, the prov-ince of Galicia or even Spain (figures 81 and 82).

Trope in the guise of contextual relevance often abandons all relevance. It fails to provide a meaningful contribution.

82. City of Culture of Galicia, Santiago de Compostela, Spain. © Bill Caplan

► HELICOPTER ARCHITECTURE –
Altering Sense of Place

A proliferation of mid-twentieth-century International Style buildings spreads the seeds of placeless architecture worldwide. Boxes of glass, steel, stone and concrete devoid of national, local or cultural context became the new symbol of modernism – architecture suitable anywhere and reflective of nowhere. Commenting on the "tasteless techno-kitsch" of Abu Dhabi's towers in the desert and the like, Ada Louise Huxtable's *Wall Street Journal* critique (2008) titled such building "helicopter architecture", "dropped down anywhere, delivering extreme, iconic images totally detached from place or past".[105]

Helicopter architecture is not limited to site-inappropriate sculptural envelopes: it applies to the lack of regard for mass, void or scale, to the international glass box, and to ubiquitous context lacking local references. In architecture school, the criticism "dropped in by helicopter" is the bane of student reviews.

President François Mitterrand's iconic Bibliothèque Nationale de France (Figure 83) is an example of this placeless architectural typology. Intended to catalyse

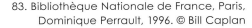

83. Bibliothèque Nationale de France, Paris, Dominique Perrault, 1996. © Bill Caplan

a new neighbourhood in an industrial area of eastern Paris, the Bibliothèque Nationale's massiveness and massive void, minimalist sterility and inaccessibility offer a cold, unfriendly environment. The influence is negative and difficult to overcome.

Placeless architecture is far more than a characterisation of corporate icons and grand statements of State. We see it emerging around the world, from London to Beijing, in numerous non-descript office and apartment buildings that also lack a sense of place, such as the apartment building in Figure 84.

Large twenty-first-century cruise ships exemplify some of the most intrusive creations of this type, placeless detached structures of inappropriate scale, in this case *floating* anywhere. Hulking 200 feet (60m) above the water line and more than 1,100 feet (330m) in length, modern ships can carry over 6,000 passengers in 2,700 staterooms plus a crew of 2,300. Bigger than any residential building in New York City in floor area or unit count, standing on their stern, they would be among the tallest. Docking in Venice, *the ship itself becomes the context*. Its mass dwarfs local character, its huge facade casts a shadow and alters the wind pattern, its emissions alter air and water quality. Four or five cruise ships in port dominate the scene, rendering the Venice experience in thousand-person swarms (figures 85 and 86).

84. This apartment building could be anywhere – it happens to be in Beijing, 2006. © Bill Caplan

85. Fourteen-storey cruise ship dwarfing
a three-storey neighbourhood in
Venice, 2014. © Bill Caplan

86. The Piazza San Marco when
cruise ships are in port, Venice.
© Bill Caplan

Saturation Breeds Change, Sometimes Unintended

When new typologies group or cluster to a tipping point, they become the norm and change the local context. This occurred with the introduction of International Style glass towers to Park Avenue in New York City: within a decade, they became the norm. The first of these glass and steel curtain-wall buildings was Lever House, completed in 1952 (Figure 87), followed by the Seagram Building and many others. Glass towers eclipsed the traditional masonry and residential nature of this area, changing it forever.

Sixty years later, a scattering of super-tall "pencil buildings", such as 432 Park Avenue, are rising above Manhattan's glass boxes between 56th and 57th Streets just north of the Lever House (Figure 88).

Nestled into a compact 93-foot-square surface area (28m x 28m), the 104 apartments of 432 Park rise 1,396 feet (426m) above the New York City streets and dwarf the surroundings (Figure 89).

Another pencil tower rises to 1,004 feet (306m) at 157 West 57th and two more are under construction, all within a few blocks along West 57th Street. 111 West 57th will reach 1,400 feet (426m) and 225 West 57th will top them all at 1,490 feet (454m). This mid-Manhattan area will reach a new tipping point before long. Skinny super-tall towers will no longer abandon the neighbourhood's context; they will define it.

Similar saturations have occurred in London and elsewhere, including a variety of typologies that characterise suburban and megacity sprawl. Neighbourhood fabric, locale and historical authenticity are increasingly on the wane, owing not only to the nature of redevelopment, but also to a lack of contextual integration.

New structures radiate an intrinsic presence that *revises physical, natural and human vectors*, whether on land or water, or perhaps airborne in the future. Absent a correlation with the site, sense of place or its ecosystem, the existence of a new entity will redefine the locale regardless of the design intent. Its mass and voids will alter the character of adjacent spaces, including the sunlight, shadow, wind squalls, water runoff, human circulation and view.

87. Lever House,
Park Avenue, NYC,
Gordon Bunshaft,
S.O.M., opened in
1952.
© Bill Caplan

88. Lever House with
432 Park Avenue
towering above at
four times the height.
© Bill Caplan

89. Super-tall 432 Park Avenue (left) rising at 1,396 feet (426m) above the NYC skyline, Rafael Viñoly. © Bill Caplan

Helicopter architecture alters context, establishing its own universe. In some instances, such regeneration is the goal, as with the Guggenheim in Bilbao. More typically, however, commercial developers and institutions tend to overlook the local consequences during design maturation, causing unintended consequences by happenstance.

The Abandonment of Context is an Obstacle to Productive Design

Even though the importance of 'context' is widely embedded in architectural education, licensure, design and criticism, a majority of architect-designed buildings seriously lack *contextual carry-through*. Many contextual references alleged during design, as well as their purported influences, are merely assertions abandoned during design execution or insignificant *gestures* to the program or surroundings. They disregard the broader aspects of the ecological triad. If you reflect on the vast majority of buildings built in almost any city or suburb within the last 50 to 75 years, this will not seem like an overstatement.

The relationships between architecture and the contexts of human ecology are inexorable, whether or not they are synergistic. Interestingly, non-architect vernacular buildings – responding to site, local customs and materials – often offer more contextual value than comparable buildings designed by architects for developers. Their vernacular character often reflects parameters such as terrain, weather, light, view and the owner's personal needs, responses developed over lengthy periods of construction and adaptation. Many developer-initiated buildings, purported to reflect context-based design, lack any local reference or relationship, ignoring sense of place as well as other references that might integrate context.

Detached from its surroundings, which include site conditions and the ecosystem as well as the reality of the program, architectural design forsakes an opportunity to afford community wellbeing, and most likely the wellbeing of the environment and its occupants. A designer's personal sensitivity to site conditions and the community is likely to add fundamental value to a design, realising true synergies. As the natural environment is crucial to human welfare, this includes attention to 'green' design as well.

Context includes the forces of nature and its resources, as well as site infrastructure, built environment, community, culture and program. All of these factors are key components of human ecological design.

▶ FUNCTIONAL AESTHETICS –
Performing Art

We experience architectural expression from up close and afar, most intimately when personally involved. We respond to the qualities of the whole *and* its parts, which become more apparent in close proximity at street level, approaching an entryway, or noticing interior features. The architecture and its purpose are evident in large and small scales, a building's entirety and its detail. Both large and small components can perform multiple functions.

Architecture's *gestalt* emerges from the arrangement and integration of its components' qualities. Likewise, the *gestalt* of each component emerges from the qualities of its materials and configuration. The components and assemblages exchange energy, influencing its distribution and emission to the environment, altering the flux that stimulates human perception. As this includes *ornamental* and *decorative* components, they too have the potential to benefit human ecological design.

Expressive elements can fulfil performative and structural roles by agency of their surface, substance and arrangement. Those executed by virtue of their material substance can function as structure or skin, or serve other physical functions. Aesthetic expressions executed through pattern, finish, colour or materials are intricacies that influence the dispersion or transmission of energy. Reflecting or projecting heat or light, shadow or colour or sound, they interact with environmental phenomena. Such interactions derive from the characteristics of the material properties and assembly, not from the creative expression. *Regardless of a component's primary purpose, it can afford other benefits by design.*

For example, consider surface tiling, coating or composite layering: they all possess materiality. Their visual and tactile properties provide sensory and cognitive stimulation. At the same time, their materiality can afford operative properties such as thermal mass, insulation, encapsulation, support, water repellence, solar reflection or absorption. We also employ the aesthetic qualities of colour for cognitive value. Yet, colour can be ecologically relevant to a building's design – colour can perform a function as well. White and light colours reflect the sun; black absorbs its heat. Likewise with pattern and texture: in addition to decoration, they too can enhance environmental performance.

The physical properties of an artistic design, either of the overall envelope or a constituent element, *intermingle* with its surrounding universe in multiple ways. Physical components that delineate space, defining volume and shelter, also define a building's sensible and operative interfaces with people and the natural environment. *Aesthetic components afford multiple opportunities.*

Intentionally or not, components created for their experiential impact, designed with one purpose in mind, aesthetic or otherwise, engage in other interactions as well. We can tailor their physical, sensible and operative characteristics to benefit both the human experience and the environment. Thus utilised, decoration and ornamentation can serve sensible, operative and physical functions. *Functionally sharing an architectural resource optimises design.*

Combining the material and performative applications of a building feature with its experiential characteristics, to provide concurrent affordances, is not a twenty-first-century idea. Edith Wharton and Ogden Codman promoted this notion more than 100 years ago in *The Decoration of Houses* (1897), proposing the use of "architectural features which are part of the organism of every house" for decorative purposes, rather than the "superficial application of ornament totally independent of structure".[106] The concurrent physical, operative and sensible use of openings, portals, is an example.

> In the decorative treatment of a room the importance of openings can hardly be overestimated. Not only do they represent the three chief essentials of its comfort, – light, heat and means of access, – but they are the leading features in that combination of voids and masses that forms the basis of architectural harmony.[107]

Wharton and Codman identify performative issues, that window placement affects light, ventilation and view, and perceptual/sensory facets such as a single pane versus its subdivision. They noted that subdividing a sash *maintains the opening as a part of the wall*, yet establishes "a relationship between the inside of the house and the landscape". A large undivided sheet of glass "interrupts the decorative scheme of the room"; the window no longer seems a part of the room's wall.[108]

These were not credos of early modernism seeking function driving form, or "less is more" minimalism: they expressed disdain for *superficial* ornamentation, but not for the ornamentation itself when achieved through synergetic composition.

Whether exterior or interior, aesthetic gestures and decorative elements afford performative interfaces: they are not merely architectural embellishments, they are building *components*. As such, they can address the triad of human ecology. The true value of a building component or assembly resides in its overall performance, its aesthetic expression *and* its physical or operative contribution to the building and its environment.

Regardless of its specific purpose, every component of a building's construction engages energy in some manner. It might interact with light, sound, heat, airflow,

structural forces or nature's elements as a function of its location, mass, material properties, shape, texture or colouration. Decoration, ornamentation and
aesthetic gestures are no exception. Like other materials and component, they
too engage energy vectors, influencing the local environment as well as eliciting
a human response.

The design and arrangement of materials and voids and the variation of material properties are the substance of aesthetic composition. In each case, although
the intended application is decorative, its physical properties might enhance or
hinder building performance.

Of course, some decorative elements lack significant substance, serving solely as
decoration. When material physicality is insignificant, the 'decoration' characterisation is clear. However, caution is in order. Even decorative paint may constitute
a membrane, one that can impede moisture, reflect or absorb light energy, or
absorb pollutants.[109]

While we generally think of tiling and other wall treatments as decorative wall
coverings, embellishments, in some applications they function akin to surface cladding. Polymer, ceramic and synthetic sheeting or tiles, canvas and other covering
materials can fall into this category, as well as stucco, coatings or epoxy paints.

Passive Performance from Decorative Craft

The multipurpose utilisation of decoration and ornamentation is an age-old technique in traditional Arab architecture, commingling decorative expression with
passive performative design. Although not immediately obvious, the use of tile,
carved stucco and stained glass ornamentation in a traditional Moroccan *riad*
helps mediate the thermal environment (Figure 90). Beyond the use of court-
yards, pools, fountains, shading devices and wind towers – microclimate, thermal
mass, evaporative cooling, solar deflection and natural ventilation[110] – traditional
Arab architecture utilises ornamentation as a passive means to mitigate heat and
encourage airflow.[111] In 'Environmental Sustainability in Traditional Arab Architecture' (2011), Wael Al-Masri explains that the juxtaposition of materials with
different reflective heat capacity generates gradients to enhance convection, a
means for temperature control. "The first line of heat control lies at the surface."[112]

90. Carved stucco ornamentation with adjacent tile, riad in Fez, Morocco. © Bill Caplan

Elaborate ornamental carvings such as those in Figure 91 produce a cognitive feast for the mind, expressing a high level of aesthetic energy. However, the intricate carved stucco also catalyses complex thermodynamic effects that create air currents, innately interacting as both a heat sink and scatter reflector. The depth of carving amplifies this effect. Much is happening in and around the surface and the arabesque cavities beyond the artistic composition. Wael Al-Masri noted that, like decorative stucco, elaborate stone carving and alternating layers of recessed brick increase the rate of convection heat transfer, creating a cooling effect.[113]

Natural convection occurs due to temperature differentials between the outer surfaces and the cavities' interior sculptured or offset surfaces. The outer surface temperatures rise from incident and reflected sunlight as well as heat in the air. The cavities are mostly shaded and therefore cooler. Cavity temperatures tend to stabilise due to the heat sinking properties of the structure's mass, while their surface temperatures are more unstable. These natural and ever-changing temperature differentials cause miniature turbulences to stimulate airflow. When juxtaposed with a large tiled surface, such as the panel above the arches in figures 90 and 91, larger scale temperature differentials occur, magnifying air movement and its associated cooling capability as air moves across the sunlit material.

Small, repetitive or intricate handmade patterns with irregularities, inconsistencies or imperfections are very effective. The irregular surface height and flatness of old tile patterns and mosaics perform in this manner. They also feel more energetic and emotive than machine fabricated or printed tiles with a flat surface. They evoke natural formations such as crystals, fractals and cells with random inclusions, fractures and imperfections.

Regularised, machine-made and commercial components with minimal surface variation generally provide a lesser cooling effect than irregular ones. If, on the other hand, the goal is to maximise reflection, a flat highly polished surface is optimal.

Wall treatments such as carving, Venetian plaster and texturing engage aesthetically because they both simulate and stimulate energy effects. By nature of their reflective, heat-transfer and thermal-retention properties, they can also serve as thermal insulators. The Moroccan tiled wall in Figure 92 radiates energy scattered

91. Carved stucco detail, riad in Fez, Morocco. © Bill Caplan

by light reflected from its intricate but irregular laid-by-hand surface. Cool to the touch yet vibrant and viscerally alive, the pattern, colours and reflected and scattered light conjure the imagination, affording an experiential interaction. Simultaneously, it provides a protective wall surface that includes thermal insulating qualities.

92. Section of intricate tiled wall, riad in Fez, Morocco. © Bill Caplan

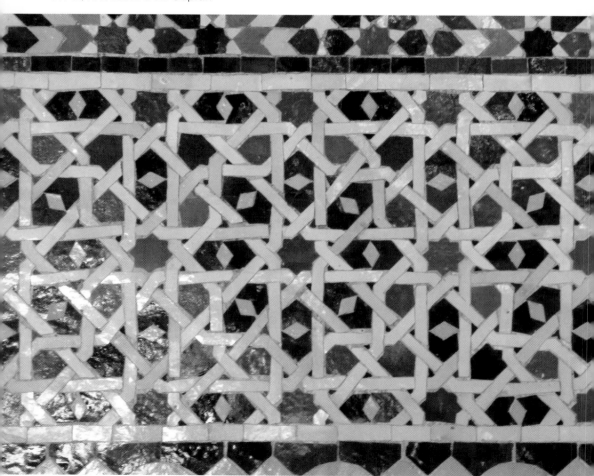

93. Selective placement of stained glass, Fez, Morocco. © Bill Caplan

Stained-glass windows are another example of expression that affords coexistent cognitive, physical and performative qualities (Figure 93). The colour, texture and patterns are highly expressive in themselves, as are the ever-changing light patterns projected by the diurnal and seasonal solar cycle. They also function as envelope barriers and sometimes ports, blocking, filtering or admitting sun, daylight, view and possibly ventilation. As thermal interfaces, their colour, surface finish and pattern interact with the incident sun.

Emitting, Reflecting and Projecting

The distinction between applied decoration, intervention and decorative architectural articulation can be subtle. Such is the case when integrating decorative images with the architecture: artwork, supergraphic wraps, lighting or embedded lights, or technology-enhanced embellishments. Embedded LED lights in wall-studded displays of static or dynamic light patterns straddle this line as well.

Architectural supergraphics are usually decorative additions to the architecture, which they sometimes obscure. As aptly put by Alvaro Viegas, "Architectural facades function as fixed skin. Supergraphics, large graphics slipped on building facades, work as clothing."[114] However, with the many new materials and display technologies available, artworks and supergraphics can materialise as an integral *component* of the skin's structure, unlike added decoration such as paint and paper. As such, when conceived as part of the skin or envelope design, these design components function as elements of the architecture.

One might draw a parallel between projected light images from an *external source* and activating *components of the skin* itself – both result in skin imagery, a source for cognitively receptive energy. There is however a difference. One is merely the *perception of a reflection*; the other derives from *an energised state* of the wall.

Active walls incorporate the means for image generation in their physicality. Passive walls are simply presentation screens, as with Doug Aitken's 360-degree exterior projections on the Hirshhorn Museum in Washington DC[115] and the Art House in Hudson Valley NY[116], cited in Sylvia Lavin's book *Kissing Architecture* (2011).[117]

The *reflections* themselves, such as those on the Hancock Tower and Seagram buildings, are not architecture (figures 11 and 15); however, the mirror-like surface finish of the fenestration is an architectural property. While the Hancock Tower's and the Seagram building's surface properties are integral with the architecture, reflecting neighbourhood images, the Hirshhorn and Art House surface images are externally applied interventions and not qualities of the architectural envelope.

We can say the same for *digital walls*: light activation is a property of the wall; the walls constitute an architectural component. Image-generating and image-reflecting properties are a distinction between physicality and phenomena.

When digital display modules comprise a curtain wall, as at Hollister California's Fifth Avenue storefront or the IAC building's interior lobby wall, both in New York City (figures 94 and 95), one might assert that the *images* displayed are part of the architecture. Here, light emission, transmission and pattern constitute qualities of the surface. Such active walls actually generate *integral surface images*, unlike passive walls that merely receive images displayed by projection.

94. Digital storefront: live feed of California's ocean surf,
Hollister California, Fifth Avenue, NYC. © Bill Caplan

95. Digital wall in the lobby of the
IAC building in NYC. © Bill Caplan

The Big Picture

The value of the experiential elements of architecture does not lie solely in their artistic merit, but in their overall synergy with both people and the natural environment. Expression offers significant value to architectural design when it adds holistically to human ecology, whether derived inherently from the building's shape, arrangement of mass, utilisation of light and shadow, or from ornament and decoration. *The parameters of human ecology consist of a matrix of contextual vectors that include the elements of expression.*

Energy, perception, the human condition, the environment, the community and their interfaces provide the parameters of engagement; the outcome will be a product of the newly built entity in all of its facets and its environment. Exploring a prospective project's human ecological interfaces will shed light on a variety of synergistic possibilities and pitfalls, lighting the way for creative *proactive design.* The physical properties of aesthetic expression are a factor in the outcome.

Performative expression and multifunction application augment design efficacy: they are important strategies of human ecological design.

4   *Architecture: Interfacing People and Environments*

Human ecological design is a *process* of creation; a process of discovery, ideation, testing and refinement. Applied to architecture, it is effectuated through the design of a building's interfaces. The objectives are to predict a prospective design's impact on people, and on the built and natural environments; to predict the impact of people and those environments on the design's efficacy; and to use that insight, to inspire the conception of synergistic architecture. The methodology requires a keen consciousness of architecture's human and environmental interactions in order to assess the *stimuli* and *effects* proactively. Human ecological design is based on a mindset, a way of thinking about architecture in terms of its interfaces and the desire *to create a built environment in harmony with people and the natural environment.*

Rather than conceive a design by contemplating line, form and shape on Cartesian coordinates in Euclidean space, human ecological design encourages creativity inspired by the forces and stimuli embodied in human ecological relationships, the enriched *vectors of influence.* Accordingly, the creative spark responds to vectors from people, the built environment and the ecosystem as well as from the program and site. Thus, human instinct and perception, local context and sense of place are incorporated. All of these vectors conjoin to stimulate design initiation and to refine design development.

Each vector is appraised for its potential impact on the design's effectiveness – its ecological interaction, experiential nature, life cycle and cost – for its potential as a resource or as a concern. Through mindfulness of the encroaching vectors and those that might emanate from the project itself, ideas emerge and solutions take shape. By anticipating each vector's influence and the foreseeable outcomes, *ideas weigh against reality*, opportunities arise for measureable results rather than token gestures. Vectors that are deemed to be significant enlighten the designer – they are *addressed with an architectural solution*.

Human ecological design is not a prescriptive process dictated by a decision tree of alternative choices; on the contrary, *the architect conceives the design*. Discovery gestates ideation. Set in motion by focusing on discreet regions of the prospective project and their corresponding site characteristics, the architect envisions form and surface in terms of human and environmental interactions. As an envelope takes shape, the scope of the focus broadens, each element is creatively refined as a component of the whole to augment both the architecture and the building's human and environmental synergies. Modelling and iterative refinement facilitate the process.

▶ THE MODEL –
Visualising Intersections

Site and building models are usually created during a project's *schematic design* after gathering information in a *pre-design* phase. Modelling is a means of consolidating the client's requirements and site information in order to explore alternative approaches to the architecture. Ultimately, a design concept emerges from the modelling process in a form sufficient for refinement during the project's *design development* phase. During development, choices are made and details are added that will drive the design's outcome, and determine its experiential and environmental viability.

Effective modelling requires numerous inputs from a range of disciplines which produce a large quantity of information. A model's utility relates to the validity of that information and the scope of its content. The need to manage such information as a resource for building design and construction has spawned an entire industry in itself – building information modelling (BIM) – an industry made possible by the computer. The art of modelling depends more than ever on our ability to parameterise this information, and to formulate parametric relationships that can guide decision making throughout the processes of design, specification, procurement and construction. 'Information' has appropriately become building modelling's middle name.

Human ecological design was characterised above as *a non-zero-sum game of synergies* (Section C.1, 'The Concepts'). *Information* intensive, the game requires a game board of information-rich interactive models. The game moves – *discovery, ideation, creation, testing* and *refinement* – develop the model through informal heuristics or complex parametric analyses. The evolving design foresees human and environmental interactions activated by architectural gestures that orchestrate a synergistic outcome.

Creating a model driven by parameter relationships facilitates the ecological design process. It enables the proactive exploration of design features and design refinements in order to finesse beneficial interventions in a creative manner. Although complex buildings require a complex computer model with highly developed algorithmic relationships, it is important to note that simpler buildings can undergo this process with less sophistication. What matters is the ability to formulate useful relationships between specific human and environmental vectors and a building's design characteristics, regardless of the model's sophistication or computerisation.

For schematic design, the initial parameters are derived from the particulars of the client's mandate and of the proposed site. The *environmental considerations*, the *local community* and the *sense of place* are all categorised as *site parameters*. Models are created to enable the visualisation and exploration of the interactive relationships among people, places, environments and the program. More important than the noting of such vectors is their transformation into quantifiable parameters in a matrix of interactive design relationships. The need to consider and quantify the effect of a design intervention cannot be overstated.

The parameters of a client's space and program requirements and those of the site are used to initiate a model. Then, vectors from the existing built environment, the natural environment, human interaction and the project itself are overlaid, vector by vector. Together, they fashion the model into an ecological design tool. With it, a building envelope and space allocation can be explored and can be conceived.

The Vectors

In the real world, each sector of the building envelope is exposed to energy and matter in various forms, both human generated and natural – *physical, chemical and radiated forces and the elements of nature.* Converging from the exterior and interior, they interact with the building envelope. At the same time, the building itself responds or emits other energy and matter. These actions and interactions can be expressed as *vectors.*

When a vector engages the surface of a particular sector, not only does the vector influence the state of that surface, the vector itself is affected. Some of the vector's energy and/or matter may be transmitted by the surface to the envelope's substance, where it will mingle with the energy/matter of the substance and from other vectors. Some of the vector's energy/matter may be transmitted completely through the envelope's section, emitted to the building's interior or exterior environment. Likewise, it might be emitted to other components of the envelope. To understand this phenomenon, visualise light impinging on a window. Some of the light is reflected at the surface; some of it passes through a pane, emerging on the other side; and some of it might scatter internally, causing the glass to glow or illuminating an edge. The same analogy applies to other components of the building envelope, even those that appear impenetrable such as walls, which are often penetrated by water, moisture, noise and heat vectors.

When an energy/matter vector has the potential to influence the condition of a building, or to influence its interior or exterior environment, it is a *vector of influence.* Whenever the building itself emits energy or matter, they too are *vectors of influence.*

As all segments of a building envelope interact with numerous forms of energy and matter, each envelope interface interacts with the parameters of multiple vectors. Each physical component interacts with other physical elements or phenomena which often include people and other living things. It is important to identify their salient interactions, to address selectively the parameters deemed important, directing the outcome of such interactions by design rather than happenstance. By focusing on specific categories of interaction, isolating relevant parameters, we can ascertain the viability of an intended design intervention. A few examples of window fenestration interactions can illustrate this concept of vector–envelope interplay.

What Are Windows For?

Originally, windows emerged as a means of allowing the passage of air, smoke, odour and light, as open holes to vent bad air and admit fresh air and daylight. Over time, a means to shield nature's elements was incorporated. In short, we think of window fenestration as a wall opening or insertion, positioned to access light and/or view and having a potential for ventilation. We punctuate an envelope with windows for these reasons. Of course, they also function as design elements as well, adhering to a designated style or aesthetic pattern, or relieving the massive feel of a large unpunctuated expanse. Thus in summary, their specifications are traditionally selected in response to the desire for daylight, view and aesthetics, and possibly ventilation. The constraints include their mode of operation and cost. With the increasing interest in green living, energy conservation has also become an important part of the selection process. As a result, the design of a building's ports requires more comprehensive thinking.

In human ecological design, fenestration, whether a window or otherwise, more than just an opening that is glazed, vented or hatched, serves a broader function as a multifunctional component of the envelope's surface. In human ecological design, windows are an element of the *envelope's interface*, part of its unified design. This concept is more obvious when we consider windows in the context of a building's cladding. Nevertheless, whether window fenestration is an integral part of a glass building's exterior cladding system or composed of individual units, *windows are a component of the envelope's surface*. Whether or not intended, windows interact with a matrix of vectors from wind, rain, noise and the sun's energy to the interior environment itself, with its own thermal profile.

The *overall impact* of a window design is not always apparent or part of the designer's consciousness – nor is it always obvious *before* installation. Under more subtle observation, a window reveals itself as a *mediator*, an interface between competing vectors and environments. Mediating one parameter often affects others.

Through the Looking Glass

Assume that a particular sector of an envelope is designated to provide an exterior view and to harvest daylight for the interior. The parameters associated with view require a scene to look at, a view corridor and a see-through port – in this case a window. Daylight calls to mind the availability of unobstructed ambient light, a favourable sun path and a light-port that can transmit natural light. Visibility from a specific interior location requires the transmission of reflected and/or emitted light from a scene. Daylight and view are the *vectors,* having both magnitude and direction in regard to their intensity, origin and path of reception. To achieve these goals, the fenestration must be designed to *transmit* both daylight and view to the interior space (Figure 96).

Transmission

Exterior Environment

Interior Space

Ambient light ⇨ ➡ ➡   daylight

Light from a scene ⇨ ➡ ➡   view

window

96. Light and view vectors.

Such site-specific and location-specific vectors can be evaluated in order to inform the envelope's design scheme and utilised to configure this portion of the building. However, daylight and view represent only two of the vectors that might be significant to this sector of the envelope. From an environmental perspective, windows do more than transmit light.

Windows are an integral part of a building envelope's surface enclosure. The probable effect of nature's elements on a building's integrity, the expenditure of energy, and interior comfort derive from other vectors that cannot be ignored, such as wind, rain and solar radiation (Figure 97). These are all parameters of significant concern. *Penetration control* is of paramount importance. Enduring shelter requires protection from the elements. Unintended penetration can catalyse material deterioration, disturb the interior climate and increase energy consumption.

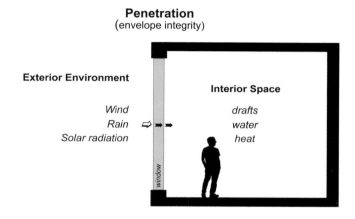

97. Penetration: undesirable vector transmission.

Fenestration's insulation value, a function of thermal reflection, thermal absorption, thermal transmission and thermal retention, plays a central role influencing the interior temperature, as does its subjectivity to wind, airflow and stagnant air masses. Fenestration designed to provide ventilation, to exhaust hot or stale air and emissions, to create airflow, or to intake fresh exterior air, also influences interior temperature and comfort level. Windows mediate temperature and can be designed to mediate air quality (Figure 98).

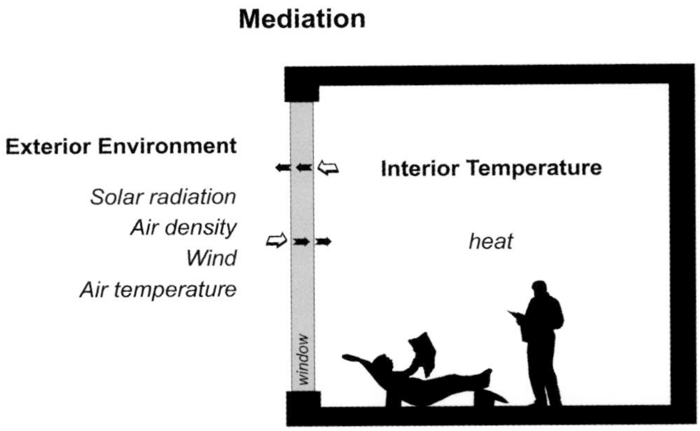

Mediation

Exterior Environment

Solar radiation
Air density
Wind
Air temperature

Interior Temperature

heat

98a. Windows mediate the influences of environmental vectors.

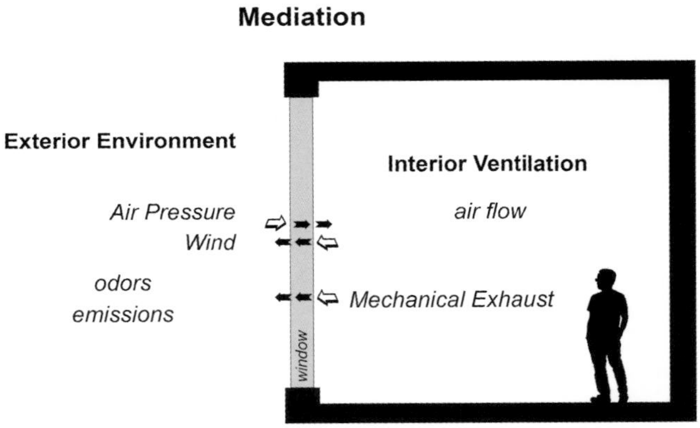

Mediation

Exterior Environment

Air Pressure
Wind

odors
emissions

Interior Ventilation

air flow

Mechanical Exhaust

98b. Windows can mediate the flow of air.

Nevertheless, while windows mediate the interior climate, their interface with other vectors can negatively impact occupants' quality of life. While ventilating an interior space to improve air quality and temperature, they also provide a path for *noise transmission* from the street. Likewise, they can transmit interior mechanical noise or human-generated sounds *to the street*, to the community (Figure 99). Attentively specified or defined, windows can mediate sound and vibration.

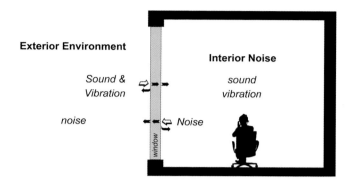

Exterior Environment

Interior Noise

Sound &
Vibration

sound
vibration

noise

Noise

window

99. Windows can mediate sound and vibration vectors.

But there is more. A building's fenestration reflects and redirects the elements of nature and human-generated sounds just as do other surfaces of the building envelope. Rainwater reflection and runoff, wind turbulence and solar reflection are notable examples of redirected vectors (Figure 100).

Reflection & Redirection

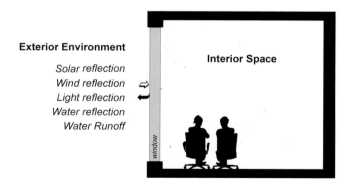

Exterior Environment

Interior Space

Solar reflection
Wind reflection
Light reflection
Water reflection
Water Runoff

window

100. Vector reflection and redirection.

With creative design, fenestration can effect, reflect, direct and mitigate other vectors such as the wind, water and solar radiation. Unintentional solar reflection is frequently underestimated during both schematic design and design development.

With the increasing use of large glass panes and glass curtain walls on tall buildings, *reflection and redirection* have become significant problems. Facade curvatures exacerbate the problem, intensifying the effects when not properly designed or perhaps not even considered. They can focus solar rays like a parabolic mirror, creating intensive heat.

In 2010, the curved glass facade on Rafael Viñoly's Vdara Hotel in Las Vegas became noteworthy for singeing a guest's hair and melting plastic bags in the pool area at certain times of the day. In 2013, intense solar reflection from the concave glass facade of Viñoly's 20 Fenchurch Street in London melted the exterior and interior plastic trim on parked automobiles and damaged nearby stores. In 2012, Scott Johnson's Museum Tower Condominium in the Dallas Arts District caused a similar problem. Sunlight reflected from the elliptical glass facade interfered with the Nasher Sculpture Center's artwork and scorched plants in the museum's garden. The solar reflection interfered with other Dallas buildings as well. All of these problems could have been anticipated and prevented – foreseeing solar reflection and predicting its course is not rocket science.

Each component of fenestration is an integral part of architecture's external and internal envelope. As such, it is a physical component that induces a broad range of influences on the environment and local context, *whether or not it was intended to do so*. Not only does it reflect and project natural phenomena to the built and natural environments, a fenestration's design influences the sense of place. It projects an aesthetic, a complex vector in itself (Figure 101). The aesthetic context projects to the community, intervening in the character of the built environment and its sense of place. It interacts directly with all those in its sphere.

Projection

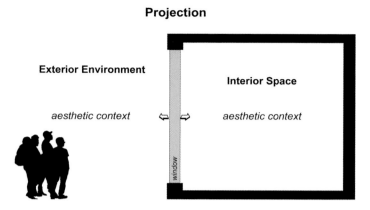

101. Vectoring sense of place.

A window's efficacy is a function of its construction: the number of panes, the gas or vacuum employed between the panes, emissivity, reflective coatings, frame and glazing-spacer conductivity, and air-tightness. A designer's choice usually concentrates on specifying heat loss (U-value), visible light transmittance (VT) and the solar heat gain coefficient (SHGC). Fenestration design or selection is often a balancing act between choosing active and passive techniques to achieve climate control and energy conservation while meeting the aesthetic require-ment, construction budget and projected operating cost. However, fenestration size, placement, arrangement and orientation also govern their efficacy.

Nevertheless, rarely can a single fenestration solution provide a sufficient balance of light transmission, insulation, solar heat gain and glare in all seasons, or in all orientations. This seems obvious, yet a single fenestration type is often specified for large parts of a building, or even its entirety – as with glass-clad buildings, some of which are mentioned in earlier chapters. This phenomenon applies to housing of all types as well.

Although we tend to think of fenestration in the context of a building's architec-ture and function, the design and construction of windows, doors, skylights and vents directly impacts the immediate environment and the local community as well. This occurs regardless of a building's functional intent, its overall design or operation, or its interior sense of place. As discussed above, while fenestration can transmit light, view and air, it can also port building-system noise, hot and stale air and emissions *directly to the community*, most notably to pedestrians. Such *external consequences* are frequently ignored in the design process.

Interfacial Interaction

But our interest here in *interfacial interaction* transcends avoiding unintended problems. The power of an ecological design approach lies in its ability to reveal beneficial opportunities, interventions that are not obvious, and design affordances that can enable energy conservation and harvesting. This includes aesthetic context, experiential interactions and cost. Cost is also a significant vector.

Cost is manifest in *monetary, environmental* and *human health* terms. Cost quantification is essential, not only the monetary, but the expenditure of energy and deterioration of environmental resources as well. This includes material and mechanical ageing and technological efficacy under actual site conditions. Monetarily, there are budgetary restraints on building a project, and on its eventual operating costs, maintenance and depreciation. Environmentally, there are expenditures relating to the consumption of energy and other natural resources, and the impact of emissions and pollution. This affects the life-cycle expenditures of energy and pollution associated with the mining, manufacturing, transporting, utilising, maintaining and disposing of what we fabricate – from cradle to grave. These vectors and many others influence the cost of human health, both physical and mental, from the impacts of building construction and operation, to a building's impact on the community and the ecosystem.

This limited discussion regarding a few of the vectors that influence fenestration performance highlights some of the areas of concern. The design parameters that cause a problem – that reflect or concentrate the sun's light and heat, that cause rainwater runoff, initiate air squalls or transmit or amplify sound and vibration – whether functional or merely aesthetic, can often be *utilised to achieve positive gains*. We can address them proactively to optimise a design if we choose. Such issues apply to all facets of the building envelope – all surfaces and substances, ports and barriers, masses and voids; they apply to their orientation, shape, volume and physical properties. As can be seen in the fenestration examples above, the characteristics of a window alone can significantly impact a building's fruitful operation, whether for the owner, the people sheltered, the community or the natural environment. This does not apply solely to fenestration, all the components of a building are impacted in the same or similar manner. Their operational efficacy lies in material selection, design configuration and the creative talents of architects and engineers.

Vectors which impact or embody experiential and environmental phenomena are enriched *vectors of influence*. The forces they represent activate the ecological model, and when addressed enable human ecological design. Good design practice seeks to identify these enriched vectors and actively deploy them to create synergies, not only with the terrain and infrastructure, but also with the local built environment and with people. Good practice strives to build a performative building envelope, one in which aesthetic characteristics are designed with environmental performance in mind. It seeks to achieve substance over tinsel; although when glitter is the goal, good practices nevertheless create tinsel *with* substantive value. Vector-influenced design can transform an outcome resulting from happenstance into an outcome resulting from intent. We must never lose site of the sectors, the components themselves or their unified design. We must never lose sight of the matrix of parametric vectors. No matter what the design aesthetic, successful architecture must addresses the reality of *interfacial interactions*.

► MODELLING BY SECTOR

How do we model the intersection of the numerous vectors that envelop a site, and that emanate both inward and outward from its architecture? The process starts during the initial development of a schematic design, as early as possible. The analysis starts with a *region* of the *site*, progresses by *sectors* of the region and finishes with specific architectural *components*. In other words, first focus on a geographic region of the site and a vague preconception of the intended building envelope. Next, envision a portion of the conceptual envelope in that region and model its interface with selected vectors of interest within that sector by addressing their parameters. Through this process, conflicts and the potential for synergies will emerge and design goals can be considered.

Envisioning an envelope's form in the context of its interior space allocation and adjacent site characteristics inevitably leads to *sector thinking*, dividing the envelope into sectors for ease of analysis. For example, designate the entrance area, or a portion of the facade or its fenestration, as an individual sector. Address it as a surface that interacts with the vectors and that projects its own vectors. Here the opportunities for ecological synergies arise. Overlap appropriate vector relationships between the envelope and environmental factors sector by sector, illuminating the challenges and opportunities with orientation and scale. Designate design goals for specific sections of the envelope's surface, ultimately to be resolved by its individual components through multifunctional interventions. Developing a design by sectors, thinking in terms of their interfaces, provides the flexibility of local specialisation needed to achieve substantive gains on a local level and to avoid the mishap of negative interactions.

Details of the client's program and budget, site topography and features, zoning and codes, climate and solar orientation, infrastructure and surroundings and the community all join forces in schematic design modelling. Whatever one's creative approach or strategy to gestate architectural form and rationale, doing so with a consciousness of human ecological interactions by sector leads to productive synergies. Once aware of a potential path for blinding sunlight, the impetus to avoid its damaging effects through creative design is instinctive. One does not need a prescribed 'sustainable design objective' to tackle such a problem proactively. Installing tack-on shades as corrective action after occupancy would be less effective. In some circumstances, early consideration of such a solar hazard might ideate an opportunity to harvest solar radiation for heat or electricity generation. Influencing the gestation of shape by orienting a facade or roof sector for such a purpose during schematic design will produce a more effective result than adding solar collectors to a non-contextual design on a fully developed envelope.

The ecological process is initiated by conceiving a project in broad terms in order to develop ecological goals, conceptualising the design in the framework of real-world experiential and environmental conditions. As ideation develops, it is tested and refined to synergise with reality on a local scale. This *iterative* process responds to the influences anticipated from without and within, both physical and experiential. As the schematic model matures by focusing on specific components and their interplay, each one is evaluated and optimised to synergise with the vectors chosen and define their interfacial interactions. The fate of the design will reside in the details of design development, where intent can succumb to standardisation or misinformation without attentive carry-through.

The physical realities of a site and its environmental properties establish the universe in which the project will emerge (figures 102, 103 and 104). They include the characteristics of the natural environment and the character of the built environment and the community. As the architect's vision forms, as masses and voids assume surfaces that define areas and volumes, their interfaces with this universe emerge. In these early stages of development, attending to ecological interactions by sector proves highly effective.

102. Site model rendering for a design competition. © Bill Caplan

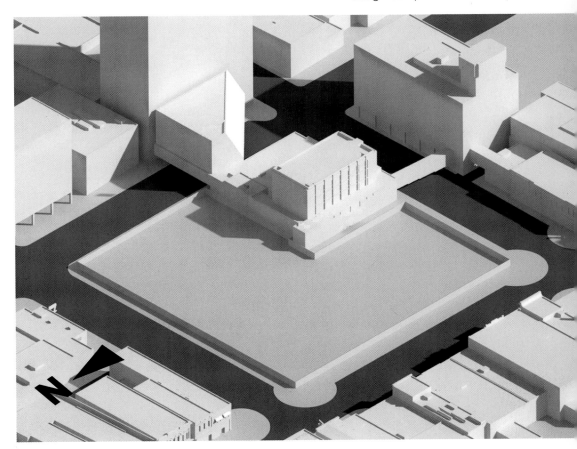

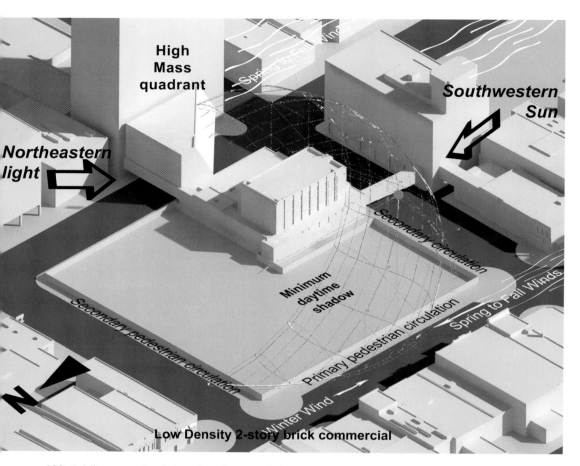

High
Mass
quadrant

Southwestern Sun

Northeastern light

Spring to Fall Winds

Secondary circulation

Secondary pedestrian circulation

Minimum daytime shadow

Primary pedestrian circulation

Spring to Fall Winds

Winter Wind

N

Low Density 2-story brick commercial

103. Adding experiential and environmental
vectors to the model. © Bill Caplan

104. A model developed by sectors
in response to the vectors.
© Bill Caplan

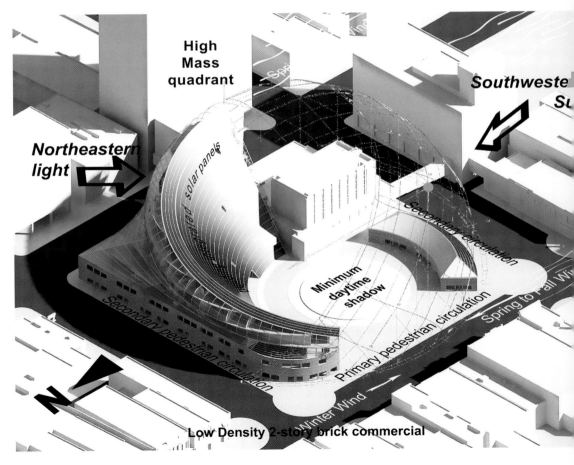

Staying the Course

The analysis of site and environmental characteristics is usually performed in conjunction with site surveys and early planning. But as a design matures, as detailing and material specification progress, the properties of those characteristics are less evident, as is the design logic that addressed them. As more architects, designers, interns, drafts-persons and consultants participate in detailing the final design, knowledge of the scheme's relationship to specific vectors and their influence on the initial design grows more distant, and is often lost. While the abstractions of plan, elevation and section develop specificity and detail, specificity and detail often overtake the design process – the tail wags the dog. Goals that initially drove a design gesture can succumb to the benefits of component standardisation, expediency, lack of technical understanding or a detailer's aesthetic execution. This is most often seen when the aesthetic detail or cost savings undermine design functionality. Unfortunately, the vectors that informed the design still matter; once forgotten or ignored, the building's functional outcome is more subject to happenstance. In the normal course of design development, specification and construction, effective responses to environmental vectors are likely to dwindle.

Conforming to site, zoning and code constraints and the client's requirements is always the overriding rule of thumb. Floor plan and circulation concepts are subsequently adjusted to fit such constraints and other practicalities to make them work, by means of rearranging, rescaling and resizing. Oftentimes, elevations are thematic or derived from an architect's pattern books. Interfacial development and its potential synergies generally suffer deferring to the overall determination of floor plans, sections and aesthetics. Designing a home for a private client is the most frequent exception, where a plan often emerges in harmony with the experiential elements of the site. Human experience takes precedent, influencing every stage of design from early conception through detailing. Yet, although green design may be one of the mandates, it often yields to experiential values, opening the door to gratuitous green solutions that feel good, rather than substantive sustainable construction and operation.

Residential subdivisions fare less well from a human perspective. Though the interiors are designed with people in mind, with limited budgets, plan and interior features usually prevail over responsiveness to the site and sustainability:

saleability rules. Multi-unit affordable housing projects, especially in urban areas, typically fare the worst. Their design and construction emerges by puzzling space, codes, zoning and program requirements to maximise the rentable space with minimum construction cost. Cost and potential income control the design process: profitability rules. Exceptions notwithstanding, experiential and sustainable design in affordable housing becomes relegated to an afterthought. Nevertheless, profitability and saleability do not automatically negate experiential and sustainable design in suburban subdivisions or affordable housing. Their lack is more a function of the design process than tight budgets.

A design process that develops from the inside out, focused on manipulating space allocations without relating to the site, and one that designs elevations without regard to environmental and experiential considerations, is bound to miss the mark. Predetermination of tectonic boundaries without such considerations precludes the opportunity to orient and shape the envelope to develop environmental and human synergies. Environment-friendly and human-friendly design merely requires the desire to do so, consciousness of the site and its surroundings, and a willingness to work the design process holistically from both inside out and outside in. With forethought and creative design, this can be accomplished despite a tight budget. That is what architects and engineers are trained to do. It is a matter of staying the course.

The Whole and its Parts: Macro–micro Thinking

A building envelope is a composite of numerous parts. Their *physical, sensible* and *operative* manifestations provide a wealth of design opportunities limited only by the architect's creativity and the engineer's toolset. The distinct characteristics of all their manifestations exist concurrently. Although each building component is an assembly composed of discreet parts, each assembly functions in its entirety as a purposeful component. It interacts directly or indirectly with the interior or exterior environment as well as with other components, and contributes to human perception. Building *sectors* are created from an assembly of components; working together they function as a unit. Yet each component itself is designed to serve a specific role. When we contemplate a building sector or the building as a whole, we *think macro*; when we analyse a component or its discreet parts, we *think micro*. Successful modelling requires both.

Models are developed iteratively, from the rough expression of the ideation through the detailing of its materiality and interactions. Surfaces are first conceived to address the program boundaries and other client mandates; they are envisioned as barriers and ports to articulate space, access, circulation and connectivity. Grouped together, the barriers and ports form sectors. Each sector, as well as each of its individual components, constitutes a part of the building envelope and contributes to the building's performance. Their arrangement will articulate the aesthetic. Every surface and substance will interface something – another surface or substance, an environment or an element of nature, the program or the sense of place, the community, the built environment or the people who experience the building. Specifying the substance of each surface will define its properties and determine its potential. *In the ecological model, operative ability and interactive influence must never be out of mind*, and will be determined by the specifics of each component's design.

Model development in human ecological design is *not* a linear process, one that addresses conceptual, programmatic, spatial, aesthetic, experiential and environmental design parameters in a step-by-step progression. As each component of the model has *multiple interfacial manifestations*, it is able to serve more than a single function at any given time by the creative employment of its material characteristics, finish and form. Therefore, from the design perspective, by investigating each component relative to its potential for multiple interactions, numerous secondary interventions can be considered while addressing the component's primary function. Creative multitasking drives the ecological design process.

Simply put, consider a component's reason for being, then explore other roles that it might perform that could be beneficial to the project. Take advantage of its properties, or of design tweaks, to add other benefits that can optimise building performance. Proactively refine the design without relegating secondary ecological interactions to future detailing, where such interest may or may not arise. Ecological refinement should be performed during each iteration of the design, employing a *macro–micro* methodology that considers both the whole *and* its parts, both primary function *and* incidental interactions.

With this approach, always think of the building as a place for people; always envision its existence and performance through the lenses of architecture and engineering, and the holistic lens of human ecology. As the envelope assumes form, as surface areas and volumes are assigned to address specific functions, scrutinise their exterior and interior interfaces to unveil both issues and opportunities. Every interfacial interaction offers an opportunity for creative utilisation.

Human ecological design, a proactive process, evaluates this matrix of vectors with an eye toward problematic interactions and productive synergies. Thus, rather than position windows solely to provide daylight or view to an adjacent program space, or to allow for fresh air or ventilation, evaluate them as a port able simultaneously to transmit, filter, repel and redirect energy and matter. Assess them as elements of the envelope's surface and substance, whose surface and substance will interface with the program, the view and the interior climate, the wind, rain, noise and the sun's energy. Assess their interfaces with people on the street and community experience. The holistic design approach queries: *What else can this fenestration do* aside from admitting daylight and view in an energy-efficient manner consistent with the budget? *Are there human ecological issues* that can be dealt with proactively, such as reflected light, noise emission, wind squalls, runoff or aesthetic context?

Evaluating building components in this manner – as active interfaces – will reveal opportunities to enhance their ecological and experiential value. In the above examples regarding window interactions, managing ambient daylight and direct sunlight is a broad task in itself. Porting daylight and simultaneously managing glare are competing parameters, as are daylight and the sun's infrared heat or damaging ultraviolet radiation (UV), which are less frequently considered. From the ecological perspective, a window is an *interfacial system* to be fine-tuned, to reflect, absorb, filter, pass or radiate different forms of energy. When an envelope interacts with diffused daylight and direct solar rays, the parameters of interest – natural light, view, infrared, UV radiation and glare – have magnitude and direction to consider; but there are other parameters to consider as well. Do we want to maximise or minimise the exterior view from within? What about the interior's visibility from the outside? Is interior daylight desirable? Is interior glare an issue or is solar reflection problematic? Should we reflect the sun's infrared heat to reduce the need for cooling, or transmit it to the interior to absorb and re-radiate for warmth? Should we reflect the interior heat back inward for conservation? Should the window assembly itself store heat? Will the occupants be exposed to harmful UV radiation and will UV rays deteriorate interior paint, fabrics, plastics, photographs and artwork?

Modern windows are systems whose design and material specifications can manage all of these vectors. Effective application will result from the architect's design intent as detailed in conjunction with an engineer's expertise. Schematic design will lay out that intent; design development will flush out the methodology and specifications – the toolset, materials and technology. This incorporates placement and orientation, and the use of shades or screens, wavelength filters such as those in low-e glass, thermal breaks, multiple-pane construction, films and coatings and the pane and face on which they should reside. All of these design options must be considered simply to *manage* the reception of natural light, view, infrared and UV radiation. However, these same window assemblies can also be designed to manage ventilation and airflow, wind and rain redirection, vapour retardation, noise transmission, electricity generation, heat storage, pollutant absorption or neutralisation, and self-cleaning.

The materials and design gestures that are able to influence these parameters can foster environmental synergies that benefit interior comfort, energy conservation, the natural environment and the surrounding built environment. At the same time, they can creatively enhance experiential parameters including aesthetics and the local context. Arrangement, form, size, shape, orientation, materiality and construction all influence the human experience. Surface and substance are physical features with performative capabilities and sensible characteristics. They are integral components of the building envelope in all of its manifestations.

When an envelope is punctuated with windows to provide daylight and view adhering to aesthetic constraints, the secondary considerations are often left to a sequential detailing process further along in design development and material specification. The ecological approach to design, conversely, considers both primary and secondary interactions at all stages of design iteration. Fenestration is always envisioned multi-functionally, as a party to a variety of experiential and environmental interactions, not just as a port for light and view. As such, the designer explores a window's physical, operative and sensible facets, its entire role in the sector. From a port's first conception, its first inclusion in the model, its exposure to the exterior and interior vectors is surveyed. This includes the aesthetic intervention and the port's potential impact on the surroundings. Heat and sound transmission, ventilation, wind, rain and solar reflection are considered at each stage of design development, in addition to the primary roles of daylight and view transmission. Ecological design employs a holistic approach to each component's functionality from the start.

Holistic by Component, by Sector, by the Entirety

The holistic mindset overviews each building sector during each stage of schematic design and design development, solidifying a unified approach to design. The vector matrix is always in mind, always a part of the model. Vectors are addressed as design parameters from the outset and during each stage of development, rather than being left for late-stage modifications or tack-on additions. Sector components, such as windows, are modelled in all of their manifestations, and as many interfacial modes as are foreseeable are scrutinised. How does it function as a surface, as a substance, as skin and/or structure, as a barrier and/or port? How does it designate space, mediate the interior and exterior climates, and influence the sense of place? Can we employ size, shape, orientation, materiality, technology and arrangement to refine its performance while maintaining the design's aesthetic integrity and budget?

The human ecological model develops through the resolution of its interfacial relationships, by resolving the intersection of the impinging vectors though creative design, and by activating *physical, sensible* and *operative* properties. The designer can enrich the ecological potential of architecture and its economic potential by modelling the affordance value of an envelope's ports and barriers, discovering the interactions they can provide. Benefits synthesise from the creative materialisation of the design, the skilful utilisation of its surfaces and substance. This can be achieved only through modelling. Successful modelling requires experiencing the site, encountering relationships with the existing built environment and the community – relating to their parameters and interfaces region by region, sector by sector. Successful modelling requires first-hand knowledge, which can be derived only from site visits by all those involved in the design, detailing and engineering processes. This holds especially true in the design development phase, where an attention to seasonal changes in the site's environment can significantly impact the efficacy of the design. Multiple visits are necessary. When a designer or detailer lacks personal realisation, mistakes are more probable and opportunities are missed.

Opportunity and Avoidance

The ecological design process addresses opportunity and avoidance, seeking to discover interactions that can be managed for benefit while eluding those that are troublesome. But more importantly, human ecological design seeks to avoid causing negative interactions. No one tries to create harmful interactions, yet they are not uncommon.

There are numerous examples from the last thirty years of high-profile architecture that has resulted in problematic designs. They include the above-mentioned Rafael Viñoly Vdara Hotel in Las Vegas and 20 Fenchurch Street in London, the Scott Johnson Museum Tower Condominiums in Dallas and the Morphosis Architects Gates Hall at Cornell University (figures 59–62). It is interesting to note that solar rays plagued all of these buildings. Yet the sun's path is entirely predictable and easily modelled, as is solar reflection and transmission. So how does this happen to high-profile, high-budget architecture that is designed and detailed by a team of seasoned architects, engineers and detailers?

Perhaps at some point in the design, engineering, detailing or material specification, awareness of the sun's scorching rays waned. Perhaps solar rays were addressed by design gestures in early development that were unintentionally altered by design refinements later in the process. Perhaps more site visits would have better illuminated the potential problems. Somehow, significant design errors occur at various scales that impact a building's ecological viability. It is amazing how many rooftop solar-panel installations are shadowed by trees, other buildings or rooftop overhangs at various times during the day or in certain seasons. Yet although a straightforward application, this also occurs commonly. Clearly, important inputs come to be overlooked.

The fact that all of these problems could have been avoided is noteworthy. A more informed material selection, surface finish or orientation could have averted the damaging reflection. In the case of Gates Hall, the artistic composition of the sunscreen array may have lost sight of the glass facade's directional exposure to the sun. On Jean Nouvel's Institute du Monde Arabe in Paris (figures 56–58), although kinetic architectural sunscreens were a forward-thinking innovation, perhaps more focus on maintenance and life cycle would have increased the probability for successful operation or altered the design completely. The design intentions for Gates Hall and the Institute du Monde Arabe were well founded, yet their outcomes failed to achieve the full benefit anticipated, thereafter creating an avoidable problem.

It is unclear whether the outcomes in these examples derive from a loss of focus or an unforeseen reality. Either way, modelling the envelope's environmental interfaces by region and sector, articulating each parametric relationship at *each* stage of design and specification, will enable opportunities and cautions to be addressed as they arise. This is the proactive path toward effective design.

Focusing on site topography, nature's elements and the adjacent buildings in order to discover synergies on a *broad ecological basis* is not the norm; it is a big picture concept relegated to a small number of concerned developers, corporations and private clients. Unless an agenda or operating budget requires energy-saving features or a focus on sustainable design, tying design to ecological synergies is not generally of concern. But even when it is, while a design review focuses directly on the program or the aesthetics, or the maximisation of space or the budget, its field of vision is temporarily *limited* and ecological synergies are generally out of mind. This is a normal occurrence. Ecological design does not automatically pervade all stages of design development. Fostering synergies and actually achieving them during operation requires a high visibility of the ecological vectors in all phases of the design/build process – schematic through final detailing, the creation of construction drawings, material procurement and construction. The root of many design failures is traceable to material substitution or replacement *after its initial specification*.

Synergistic opportunities and areas of concern are easily identifiable while analysing a proposed design intervention with the site's topography, nature's elements and the adjacent buildings, assessing the reality of each influence. Although such analysis is normal protocol during schematic design, the focus is primarily on space-use designation, layout and flow, infrastructure, daylight allo-cation and stylistic theme; environmental and experiential interactions are not necessarily part of the assessment. As a result, the opportunity to include them in a design's DNA is easily overlooked. Modelling intersections with a vector matrix of significant parameters from the start is a key to achieving the design goals and avoiding the pitfalls. The process requires constant visibility of the real interacting phenomena and their interfaces with each component of the building.

The following case studies of built architecture demonstrate this creative approach, seeking ecological opportunities by addressing aesthetic experience, green construction and sustainable design concomitantly. They are buildings that care about people and our ecosystem; aesthetic experience, green construction and sustainable design are part of their DNA.

▶ CASE STUDIES

The Stradella Road Residence by David Hertz, 1998[118]

Architect David Hertz's client wanted a residence built in Los Angeles, California that was both "aesthetically harmonious" and "environmentally sensitive".[119] Hertz approached those goals holistically, with great attention to the design of the details relative to their role in the building envelope's performance. Both the detail and the entirety are especially sensitive to the site's experiential and environmental vectors. Green design, sustainability, human comfort and aesthetics make up the DNA of each building component as well as their composite (Figure 105).

In macro view, the envelope's design response to the site's experiential and environmental vectors is immediately apparent, whether from the prospective of architecture or though the holistic lens of human ecology. In the micro view, through the lens of engineering, the quest for a healthful and sustainable design is evident in the details.

The site vectors offered unobstructed views from the north and east, excellent north-eastern light, an opportunity for northern shade and a cool prevailing breeze that could assist natural ventilation. Street proximity, an adjacent residence and solar radiation were vectors to contend with. Through modelling, the exterior envelope was designed to orient its surfaces, volumes and ports in harmony with sun's diurnal and seasonal paths, and to take advantage of shading, the prevailing breezes and the expansive view. The interior volume was modelled to analyse the

105. Eastern facade of the Stradella Road residence by David Hertz. Thermal chimney in centre. © Bill Caplan[120]

airflow, heat flow and light distribution in order to develop an environmentally efficient scheme for climate control and the use of natural light. The architects worked closely with the Carrier Corporation to develop room volume and flow configurations in conjunction with a site-specific, zoned climate-control system.

Sector by sector, each component of the envelope or its systems was developed in conjunction with the operation of the whole. As the schemes for climate control and daylight access emerged, they were achieved by co-opting the building's surfaces, substances, volumes and orientations for multiple purposes.

Architectural creativity, a healthful environment and environmental sustainability were components of the parametric matrix.

The architects created two towers as key components in the climate control plan to function as thermal chimneys. The primary tower, 40 feet (12m) in height, doubled as the main stairwell in addition to serving its climate control function. It also included an elevator cage. To allow for the free flow of air and rising heat, the stairs and cage were constructed with perforated steel, woven-wire fabric and mesh (figures 106 and 107).

106. Perforated steel stairs, woven-wire elevator cage, Stradella Road residence.
© Bill Caplan

107. 40-foot thermal chimney tower with stair and elevator, Stradella Road residence.
© Bill Caplan

This is a good example of designing surfaces and substances to afford multiple functions, in this case as supporting surfaces and barriers that port air and thermal currents.

Recovering heat from the living room and master bedroom, a mechanised skylight evacuates the hot air during the summer. Accumulating hot air above the second floor, the tower's design allows the vent to be open while the air conditioning is cooling below, without a significant impact on performance. In winter, rising heat is captured for recirculation through a hot-air recovery system-return situated beneath the skylight. Additionally, large windows in the tower bring light and view to the stairwell as well as to the first and second floors; glazed with high performance low-e glass, the sun's infrared heat is reflected. Operable transom windows and large door openings take advantage of the prevailing breeze and allow for increased airflow to assist climate control.

108. Wall openings venting hot air to the tower, Stradella Road residence. © Bill Caplan

Additionally, wall openings were strategically placed to vent heat from the living room and master bedroom to the tower (Figure 108). On the macro level, the tower itself serves the dual purpose of people circulation and thermal chimney.

By utilising open steel and wood floor trusses between the first and second floors, the resulting cavity serves as a large return-air plenum for the HVAC system. Not only does this allow for easy air movement, it eliminates the need for a network of in-wall return ducts or soffits. Utilising the space between the ceiling and the floor above for this additional function reduces the material requirement and cost, and the need to construct soffits that would occupy living space.

The second tower consists of a shaft running up from the first-floor kitchen through the second floor to a rooftop skylight vent. It serves multiple functions as a light shaft, heat chimney and air exhaust. The skylight ports light to illuminate the bedroom area as well as the kitchen. The shaft's partially frosted glass walls amplify the illumination effect while maintaining the open feeling of the floor plan. The shaft contains the winter heat-recovery return ventilators for the kitchen (figures 109 and 110).

Light shafts are strategically located around the house, especially where privacy is desired adjacent to the adjoining property. The use of light shafts, such as those behind the table in Figure 111 is another creative means to provide the benefit of natural light experientially, thereby reducing interior lighting energy consumption.

Another interesting environmental feature is the heat sinking wall. A large curved exterior wall from front to rear threads the residence's interior, bifurcating the home into public and private spaces. The wall bounds the second-floor hallway. Surfaced with steel-trowelled black cement, it functions in a manner similar to a 'trombe' wall by collecting solar heat during the winter. A trombe wall slowly absorbs solar radiation during the day, radiating the heat to the room at night. The curving black wall is energised by the low winter sunlight that passes through the floor-to-ceiling window at the end of the corridor. In order to maximise solar heat transmission to the interior in this location, which faces southwest, this window does not use low-e glass. The solar infrared heat is not reflected. The wall curvature along the hall subjects a large portion of its surface area to the sun's infrared

109. Kitchen: light shaft, exhaust and heat chimney, Stradella Road residence. © Bill Caplan

110. Light shaft through the second floor with thermal-recovery ventilator. © Bill Caplan

111. Floor-to-ceiling light shafts.
© Bill Caplan

112. Detail of left light port and shaft in
Figure 111. © Bill Caplan

rays. The black cement pigmentation and surface texture assist heat absorption. Both the radiant heat gain from the window and the heat retained by the black wall contribute to winter comfort and reduce the need for heat generation (Figure 113).[121]

In order to manage seasonal heat gain or loss through the large picture windows (Figure 105), high-performance low-e reflective glass was installed. This low emissivity glass contains a coating that selectively reflects portions of the solar wavelength spectrum to reflect infrared light. During the summer months, the low-e coating reflects the solar infrared, minimising heat transmission through the large windows; during the winter heating season, it reflects interior heat back into the house, reducing heat loss. Extended roof overhangs partially shade the windows from the high summer sun, providing an additional benefit.

The Stradella Road residence contains many more design elements that bring together physical, sensible and operative properties that contribute to its human ecological design. As they are too numerous to discuss here, I will mention only a few which, in conjunction with their experiential value, are either environment friendly or address human health. With an architectural creative gesture, the architects cantilevered the second-floor master bedroom to extend outward, enveloped by a canopy of mature pine trees. Although the bedroom comes close to the tree canopy, by cantilevering, it does not disturb the tree's roots. Recycled timbers were used throughout the house for conservation and zero-VOC paints were used to provide a healthy interior environment (no volatile organic compounds). The ceiling wood was finished with natural linseed oil instead of stains or varnish.

From ideation to completion, the architects, engineers, suppliers and constructors never lost sight of the desire to design and build creative architecture that was human *and* environment friendly – experiential, green and sustainable. These *design principles* are not limited to well-funded projects: they can just as easily be applied with a less generous budget.

113. Curved hallway wall surfaced with trowelled black cement; the southwest window.
© Bill Caplan

The Clark Center by Tadao Ando, 2014

Tadao Ando's Clark Center at the Clark Art Institute in Williamstown, Massachusetts embraces all the constituents of human ecological design: synergies among people, the natural environment and the pre-existing built environment. Aside from creating additional exhibition space and other facilities for the institute, the overall building plan enhanced the landscape with a series of tiered reflecting pools and public walking trails that benefit both visitors and the local community. But this is a lot more than a landscaped park, as the reflecting pools and landscaping are an integral part of a new hydrology system for the entire campus, one that significantly reduces the consumption of natural resources. The hydrology plan was developed by Reed Hilderbrand Landscape Architecture, targeting a fifty percent reduction in water use for an estimated annual savings of up to one million gallons. To achieve the goal, Ando and Reed Hilderbrand created a symbiotic partnership between the building envelope and the natural environment by coordinating the architecture and landscape designs with sound engineering practice. Aesthetics, experiential interaction, community benefit and environmental sustainability were all high priorities.

114. The Clark Center entrance, Tadao Ando, the Clark Art Institute, Williamstown, MA. © Bill Caplan

Performatively, the building envelope achieves multiple objectives that include shelter, temperature control, daylight access, storm-water runoff and water management. The in-ground design utilises the earth's thermal mass for thermal stabilisation. Excavated landscape adjacent to the lower level provides huge trough-like window wells to flood below-grade areas with natural light. The envelope was designed to harvest rooftop rainwater and snowmelt as well as foundation water, assisted by green roofs over the underground space to insulate, and to absorb and control water runoff. The parking areas are paved with a water-permeable surface that drains rainwater and snowmelt, directing it to the collection system.

Collected water is stored and re-circulated through a reservoir that feeds the reflecting pools. It is used for non-potable grey-water plumbing and irrigation, cooling-tower replenishment and recycling back to the system. Cleansed excess water can be discharged to the ecosystem. While these features are environmentally sound, they also serve an aesthetic function, which includes a beautiful water feature visible from both interior levels. The Clark Center's building envelope is not only physical and operative: its water features and overall interface with the site's landscape and ambient light afford artful experiential interaction (figures 114–122).

115. The Clark Center viewed from the Clark Art Institute campus. © Bill Caplan

116. The Clark Center hydrology
system upper-tier reflecting pool.
© Bill Caplan

117. The Clark Center ground-level
hydrology system water feature; excavated
light well in rear. © Bill Caplan

118. The Clark Center from below grade
(lower level) with light well and exterior water
feature. © Bill Caplan

119. The Clark Center's below-grade gallery
light well, situated under the green roof in
Figure 120. © Bill Caplan

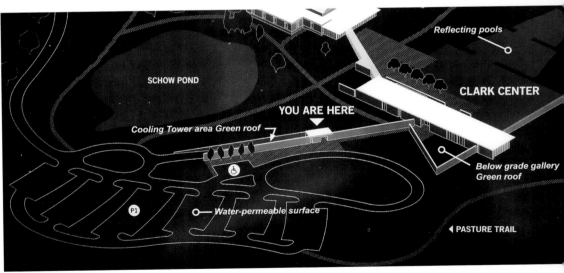

121. Above: Cooling tower area green roof. Below: Orientation display (hydrology annotations by the author).

120. A Clark Center green roof over the below-grade gallery in Figure 119; light well to the left.
© Bill Caplan

122. The Clark Center is designed for people in synergy with the environment. The reflecting pools. © Bill Caplan

As demonstrated by the Clark Center's hydrological system, individual sectors of an envelope can be designed to provide multiple functions simultaneously, such as collecting and conserving water while providing cooling, insulation and shelter, or distributing water while serving an aesthetic function. Components of a building's envelope can filter phenomena selectively – such as reflecting sunlight while transmitting view, or channelling daylight without the sun's heat. This ability to orchestrate the physical, sensible and operative nuances of built design to foster a healthful relationship between people, the built environment and the natural environment is the essence of human ecological design and the architecture it can inspire.

Sober Realities

In light of these two sound works of architecture, both human and ecologically friendly, it is sobering to consider the significant role buildings play in our health and welfare, the health of our natural environment, and their financial cost. Regardless of whether one buys or rents, housing is the most costly durable purchase made by individuals or families. It far exceeds the purchase of an automobile, appliances or technology. For people who buy, it is likely the largest such purchase they will ever make. Whether a single or multi-family dwelling, a building's lifespan will far exceed those of the others, and so will its cost in energy and pollution.

In 2010, buildings in the United States were responsible for 54% of sulphur dioxide emissions, 17% of nitric oxide emissions and for the release of 0.5 million pounds (225,000 kg) of volatile organic compounds (VOC).[122] As 0.5 to 1.5 million homes are built annually in the United States alone, in addition to commercial, industrial, institutional and government buildings, ecologically enlightened design can have a monumental impact on the viability and sustainability of our environment and human health.

According to the United Nations Environment Programme (UNEP) Sustainable Building and Climate Initiative, buildings and their attending building systems account for approximately 40% of the globe's energy consumption, 40% of its consumption of resources and 25% of global water usage. Residential and commercial buildings together consume approximately 60% of the world's electricity and emit approximately 30% of the world's greenhouse gas emissions.[123] The UNEP 2009 *Summary for Decision-Makers* concluded that "if the desired targets for greenhouse gas emissions reductions are to be met, Decision-Makers have to tackle emissions from the Building Sector with greater seriousness and vigour than they have to date."[124] More explicitly, the *pre-design, schematic design* and *design development* phases of the building design process were singled out: "decisions taken during the Feasibility Assessment and Design phases in early stages of a building's life will have a major impact on the level of emissions during the Operational Phase".[125]

The greatest energy consumption and related emissions occur in this operational phase, when a building is occupied and in use. The most cost-effective and efficient means to reduce such consumption and emission is achieved by refining the building design itself, by creatively applying building science and technology to maximise environmental synergies. This is evident even in the simplified window examples above. The embodied energy and CO2 equivalent emissions in commercial wood windows in the United States is less than half that of aluminium windows.[126] The heat loss factor (U-factor) of double-glazed windows is approximately half that of single glazing. If the budget allows, gas-filled triple glazing with a low-e coating can reduce the heat loss by up to a factor of six.[127]

It is true that the cost of energy-efficient building materials and systems can be a budgetary issue; however, as they reduce heating and cooling costs during occupancy, the gains often offset the expense. Nevertheless, creatively addressing a site's environmental vectors by configuring and orienting envelope sectors and informed material selection can substantially reduce the operating costs as well.

Given a building's long lifespan, and the magnitude of its purchase price and operating cost, shouldn't more attention be paid to the virtue of its design? Mistakes that impact the environment, a building's integrity and the welfare of its occupants can persist for a long time. They can be extraordinarily expensive to correct – if they are correctable at all.

▶ UNLEASHING THE HOLISTIC APPROACH – Human Ecological Design

There are numerous ways to assemble sticks and leaves to form a protective canopy. Likewise, there are numerous ways to engineer function and efficiency in cars, trains, planes, rockets and machines or Corbusier's machines for living.* Whatever the purpose, our material compositions are *created to serve people* in some way, whether they emerge from instinctual construction, engineering, art or craft. Each object is designed to perform within a matrix of parameters and to interface humans with an experience, energy and/or matter. Some outcomes are more effective or efficient and some are more aesthetic or creative than others. Some coffee cups maintain coffee temperature better than others; some protect

---

*   Le Corbusier writing in 1923 in *Vers un Architecture*: *"Une maison est une machine-à-habiter"* [a house is a machine for living in].

our hands from the heat. Some channel the aroma, while others prevent spills. Some are single use, some serve for a lifetime and some take generations to disintegrate in landfills. Some are utilitarian, others appeal to our senses, an experience in themselves. The same holds for buildings. They too are an interface between people and a purpose, designed to perform within a matrix of parameters; they too interface people with an experience, energy and/or matter.

Buildings are for people, they always have a purpose and they always provide interfaces among a matrix of parameters. How they look and function is a product of human design, human instinct, human choice and human perception. The parameters addressed and a building's ultimate interactions result from *the designer's actions*. A building envelope, far more than a space-occupying intervention that houses a client's program, can play a large role in the schema of human ecological architecture. The physical, sensible and operative facets of the architectural interface significantly influence human ecology, each in its own way. They conjoin in the totality of the intervention.

Historically, the shape and form of an architectural envelope was an imaginative creation conceived to achieve a designated purpose, or simply to implement a program by occupying a site's boundaries. Since the onset of this millennium, a proliferation of computer-aided processes has broadened the scope of artistic conception, enabling computational, parametric, biomimetic and other methods of form finding and environmental interface. In many cases, engineers develop form-specific building structures to enable the construction of these creations. While new building components may incorporate multi-functional interactions, such as a curtain wall that can harvest and convert solar radiation to usable energy, artistic positioning or spatial arrangement sometimes trump their operative value or function. This need not be. We have the capability to fuse aesthetics and function seamlessly through the proactive employment of building science and technology, new building materials and techniques.

Contextually integrating interface technology with architectural design is the ideal. It provides an opportunity to maximise architecture's symbioses with the community and the natural environment. Conceiving exterior and interior creations in concert with their *physical, sensible* and *operative* contexts not only defines space and sense of place, but also their human and environmental interactions.

By doing this, we orchestrate the integration of program with the users' needs, community sensibilities and environmental sustainability.

If we visualise architecture not only as physicality, but also as a product of inter-face – a system of mediation and affordance – we enable a holistic approach that can utilise computer-aided conception in this broader context, as something more than mere artistic conception. When we allow human ecological references to inform the design process, they drive the building envelope to function as both surface *and* a system of purposeful components – as barriers, filters, ports and structures – providing unity of programmatic space, environmental function and a legitimate sense of place. In this manner, the architectural interface merges and emerges as cause, effect and effecter.

Architecture draws power from the schemata of its interface, enunciated by its constituent influences of program, community, nature and the existing built environment. Achieving that power, the interface of architecture both catalyses and expresses human energy. *Architecture embodies the energy of influence.* More than a physical shelter, an assembly of functions or an artful expression, the building envelope constitutes their sum. Its surfaces, substances, barriers and ports are what afford the physical, operative and sensible qualities. Together they inter-play with people and the environment. Together they constitute the architecture. How a building looks is part of how it works, and so are its interactions with the environment.

Overall, we should regard the building envelope as this *human ecological interface,* an assembly of substances and media bound by surfaces, whose algorithmic functions provoke, facilitate and mediate environmental change and experiential activity. Whether a wall, floor, foundation, ceiling, roof or fenestration, the physical and aesthetic qualities of its interfacial interactions are always active. Each element of the envelope is an intervention that will interface in some way with the intended program, human perception and the natural environment. As such, an informed design that employs their interfacial capabilities can benefit both the client and human ecology. While such benefits might materialise by chance without conscious design, it is more likely they would not materialise at all. By design or by happen-stance, the composition of the building envelope determines the nature of these functions. Successful outcomes are more likely to occur by design.

Since the earliest days of human shelter, while the fundamental need for protection from the elements and security remained constant, an expanding purview has spawned functional enhancements such as climate control, comfort and aesthetics. Now that purview includes green and sustainable design. Fortunately, building components that function to provide shelter, access, egress, fenestration and aesthetic expression can actively serve as receptors, collectors, reflectors, filters, insulators, depots or generators. Aesthetic and functional design can be integrated. As Lance Hosey suggested in *The Shape of Green: Aesthetics, Ecology, and Design* (2012), designers everywhere can "erase the distinction between how things look and how things work".[128] This can be realised by unleashing the holistic approach though a process of proactive design iterations. Architects and engineers together can erase that distinction – by design.

Perhaps the application of such human ecological concepts seems overwhelming or impractical. However, they simply rely on the desire to achieve a people friendly and environment friendly outcome that addresses reality. Successful implementation does require one to eschew gratuitous design gestures that substantively lack their purported value, and gestures lacking preliminary site- and design-specific analysis. Successful implementation also requires a conscious proactive effort and carry-through that considers both the macro and micro views, that works detail concomitant with the entirety. Neither of those fundamentals falls out of the purview of good architectural practice, nor should they overwhelm practitioners. When human ecology is addressed from the pre-design phase and carried throughout the process, it becomes an instinctual part of design.

Human Ecological Design

Human ecological design proactively interfaces people with environments by constructing a built environment. By implementing operational details that obtain meaning from the whole, human ecological design establishes new spaces, their sense of place and their environmental interfaces.

The design and construction of the buildings in which we live, work and recreate profoundly influence human experience, health, welfare *and* environmental soundness. As demonstrated by the examples above, architecture can arouse visceral experiences and beneficial feelings while effectively performing its programmatic function, all in a sustainable manner. A sensible nature, green character and sustainable properties make buildings both people and environment friendly. Thoughtful gestures created with performative characteristics matter. They can bring life to the fabric of architecture and manage its interaction with our natural resources.

Architectural designs that merely puzzle physical, mechanical and budgetary solutions to shelter and space allocation are little more than engineered designs – technical solutions lacking ecological concerns. Architectural designs ruled by artistic expression tend to create artful sheds lacking ecological values. Many architectural installations of sustainable technology represent little more than educational demonstrations, lacking verifiable value from cradle to grave. While all of them entail significant planning effort, design development and expense, they omit *attention to the human ecological triad*: relationships among people and the built and natural environments. When integral with the design process, these factors influence those outcomes positively.

The act of building is transformational, activating the character, the physical attributes and the tenor of a space – generating the sense of place. The act of building generates a physical intervention which consumes, stores, emits and reflects a significant amount of energy, altering the energy balance with the natural environment and with the built environment adjacent to the site. Architecture interacts with our ecosystem in an ever-present interplay of energy.

Driven by the client's agenda with its goals, program and budget, the architecture can transform a space to a place in surprising ways, arousing one's mental sensibilities, emotions and sense of wellbeing. Just as we sense the energy in a leaning object or balanced rock, latency on the verge of kinetic release, we perceive the energy inherent in architectural shape, form and mass. That shape, form and mass, while providing shelter, separating space and creating environments, can also harvest solar energy, terrestrial heat, wind, rain and snowmelt, and benefit from the earth's insulation, natural shading and features of the pre-existing built environment. The more we integrate design gestures with the natural environment and its resources, and take enlightened advantage of new materials and technologies, the more cost effective and ecologically beneficial the result. Attention to these parameters and their vectors enables the principles of human ecological design to generate sound ecological solutions regardless of the budget or the size of the project. Success is about adhering to good design practice.

Creating buildings for people requires human expression and the science of environmental synergy; it requires all of the design capabilities of the architect and the technical capabilities of the engineer. Creating buildings for people requires human ecological design. *These basic premises*, although sometimes suppressed, are the foundation of architectural education around the world. Their implementation and *carry-through* will drive the practice of human ecological design. The holistic approach to design can be stated simply: *buildings are for people*.

A building for people, the Norwegian National
Opera & Ballet, Oslo, Snøhetta. © Bill Caplan

ACKNOWLEDGMENTS |

A day with the late Lawrence Halprin in 1994 fertilised the conception of this book. Larry was my wife's first cousin. Seeing the built environment through his eyes was to experience the orchestration of space, time, people and movement while addressing ecological and biological needs. Those thoughts remained with me, to use Larry's words, "smoldering and gestating for years before they erupt[ed]".* Eleven years later as those ideas coalesced, my preoccupation with building for people began. Larry, thank you for sharing your vision.

In March 2013, after a year of writing, I approached Richard Brilliant, Professor Emeritus of Art History and Archaeology and Anna S. Garbedian Professor in the Humanities at Columbia University, for his thoughts on my thesis. With numerous readings and discourse over two and a half years, his rigorous and insightful critiques were exceeded only by his encouragement and generosity. Richard, thank you for your wisdom, patience and interest.

After reading the partial manuscript in 2014, Professor Sheila Danko, Chair of the Department of Design & Environmental Analysis at Cornell University's College of Human Ecology, suggested the phrase "human ecological design". Thank you Sheila for your many thoughtful recommendations and for energising my focus on the human ecological triad – people, the built environment and the natural environment.

I wish to thank Professor Peter Macapia at the Pratt Institute Graduate School of Architecture and Urban Design for his clarity of thought, and for seeding the

---

*   Lawrence Halprin, *The RSVP Cycles: Creative Processes in the Human Environment,* Acknowledgments, George Braziller, Inc., New York, 1969.

concept of architecture as a "singularity", as an active interface. Peter, I appreciated your discerning comments during manuscript development. And thanks to Professor Ferda Kolatan for teaching the art of form-making through *iterative refinement*, to nurture its material, cognitive, visceral and performative properties – a technique implicit in the human ecological design process. Appreciation also to Professor Deborah Gans for her thought provoking and inspirational teaching of the history and theory of architecture.

I would also like to acknowledge Oliver Caplan and Christopher Beagan, who were the first to read the manuscript in its infant stage. Thank you for your illuminating comments.

Finally, last but not least, a very special thank you to Paula Luria Caplan, my wife and an urban planner, whose knowledge of planning was indispensable. Not only did she read and edit more iterations of the manuscript than I care to remember, but discussed them over every meal.

Thank you Libri Publishing and Green Frigate Books for your interest in architecture, people and the environment, and for bringing this book to print in such a short timeframe.

LIST OF PHOTOGRAPHS
AND ILLUSTRATIONS|

All photos and illustrations are by the author unless otherwise noted.

22. Apple Store, Fifth Avenue, New York City

23. Apple Store stairs, Fifth Avenue, New York City

24. Cuban National Arts School, Havana

25. A few barrier and port design capabilities illustration

26. Passing the Guggenheim Bilbao, Spain

27. Approaching the Guggenheim Bilbao, Spain

28. Norwegian National Opera & Ballet, Oslo

29. Paul-Löbe-Haus forum, Berlin

30. El Transparente altarpiece, Cathedral of Saint Mary, Toledo, Spain

31. Jewish Museum Berlin

32. Memorial to the Murdered Jews of Europe, Berlin

33. Solid cast glass, Punta della Dogana, Venice

34. Maxxi museum, Rome, Italy

35. Castelvecchio, Verona. Italy

36. Kanizsa triangle illustration

37. Illusory triangle from line terminations illustration

38. Illusory inflected contours illustration

39. Twelfth-century Modena Cathedral, Italy

40. National Ballet School of Cuba

41. Bronze doors, Museo del Prado, Madrid

42. Lava formation on Fernandina Island, Galapagos

43. Rock scree, Spitsbergen, Svalbard Archipelago

44. Iceberg, Lago Grey Peninsula, Patagonia

45. Glacial flow, Beagle Channel, Tierra del Fuego

46. Torre di Pisa, Italy

47. Intertwining spans, Passerelle Simone-de-Beauvoir, Paris

48. Passerelle Simone-de-Beauvoir, Paris

49. Skewing the dot illustration

50. Skewing the line illustration

51. Villa Savoye, France; photograph by Isabelle Lomholt

NOTES |

1 Author's 2008 conversation with the professor of an architecture history/theory seminar at the Pratt Institute Graduate School of Architecture and Urban Planning.

2 Vitruvius, *The Ten Books of Architecture*, Translated by Morris Hicky Morgan, Chapter II, p.13, Dover Publications, Inc., New York, 1960 (unaltered and unabridged republication of the first edition published by the Harvard Press, 1914).

3 Ibid., p.38

4 *Select Proceedings of the European Society of International Law*, Volume 2; 2008, edited by Hélène Ruiz Fabri, Rüdiger Wolfrum, Jana Gogolin, 30 June 2010, Bloomsbury Publishing.

5 Vitruvius, op. cit.

6 Ibid.

7 Patrik Schumacher, *The Autopoiesis of Architecture: A New Framework for Architecture*, Volume 1, p.97, John Wiley and Sons, Ltd., West Sussex, UK, 2011.

8 Ibid., p.35

9 Ibid., p.36

10 Frank Lloyd Wright, *The Art and Craft of the Machine*, Hull House lecture, 1901, reprinted in *The Essential of Frank Lloyd Wright: Critical writings on architecture*, edited by Bruce Pfeiffer, pp.24–5, Princeton University Press, Princeton, NJ, 2008.

11 Winston Churchill, addressing the Architectural Association school, 1929; *Architectural Association Journal*, 54 (May 1939), reprinted in *Architectural Association Quarterly* 5:44–46.

12 Author's Terrain House 800 concept for auxiliary housing: affordable add-on houses for the hilly terrain of Wellfleet and other Cape Cod, MA sites with minimal increase in visible density.

13 J.W. Goethe, *Letters from Italy*, available from:
http://archive.org/stream/goethesworksvol00goetgoog/goethesworksvol00goet-goog_djvu.txt
http://books.google.it/books?id=xrMUFgmurO4C&pg=PA253&lpg=PA253&dq=Goethe

14 Daniel Kahneman, *Thinking, Fast and Slow*, p.95, Farrar, Straus and Giroux, New York, 2011.

15 Chris Frith, *Making Up the Mind: How the Brain Creates our Mental World*, p.111, Blackwell Publishing, Malden, MA, 2007; noted by Eric R. Kandel in *The Age of Insight: The Quest to Understand the Unconscious in Art, Mind and Brain, from Vienna 1900 to the Present*, Random House, New York, NY, 2012, p.234.

16 Kandel, op. cit., pp.200, 234

17 Richard L. Gregory, *Eye and Brain: The Psychology of Seeing*, Fifth Edition, p.244, Princeton University Press, Princeton, NJ, 1997.

18 Peter Zumthor, *Thinking Architecture*, p.77, Birkhäuser, Basel, Switzerland, 2010.

19 Francis Crick, *The Astonishing Hypothesis: The scientific search for the soul*, pp.25–6, Touchstone Edition, Simon & Schuster Inc., New York, 1995.

20 Kandel, op. cit., pp.233–4

21 Crick, op. cit., p.143

22 Ibid., p.151

23 Richard L. Gregary, *Eye and Brain: The Psychology of Seeing*, pp.75–6, Princeton University Press, Fifth Edition, 1997, and Kandel, *The Age of Insight*, op. cit., pp.261–2.

24 Kandel, op. cit., pp.341 and 345

25 Ibid., p.345

26 Ibid., pp.355–8

27 Ester Thelan and Linda B. Smith, *A Dynamic Systems Approach to the Development of Cognition and Action*, p.180, MIT Press, Cambridge, MA, 1994, first MIT Press paperback edition, 1996.

28 Ibid.

29 Gregory, 1997, op. cit., p.2

30 Crick, op. cit., p.25

31 Richard Gregory, *Seeing Through Illusions*, p.211, Oxford University Press Inc., New York, 2009

32 Drawn by the author, based on the Kanizsa triangle and a figure from Crick, op. cit., p.47.

33 Gregory, 2009, op. cit., p.213

34 John Allman, *The Origin of Neocortex*, p.260, Seminars in THE NEURO-SCIENCES, Vol. 2, 1990: pp.257–62, *From the Division of Biology*, 216–76, California Institute of Technology, Pasadina, CA 91125, USA.

35 Lawrence Halprin, *The RSVP Cycles: Creative Processes in the Human Environment*, p.104, George Braziller, Inc., New York, 1969.

36 Le Corbusier, *Towards a New Architecture*, p.1, translated from the thirteenth French edition by Frederick Etchells, Dover Publications, New York, 1986, originally published by John Rodker, London, 1931.

37 Shan-Tung Hsu, *Tao of Feng Shui - Book One: The Fundamentals of Feng Shui*, p59, Blue Mountain Feng Shui Institute, Seattle, 1999.

38 Ibid., p.89

39 Ibid., p.65

40 Ibid., pp.62–3

41 Vincent Scully, note to the second edition of *Complexity and Contradiction in Architecture* by Robert Venturi, p.11, Museum of Modern Art, New York, second

edition 1977, reprinted 2002.

42   Zumthor, op. cit., p.77

43   D'Arcy Wentworth Thompson, *On Growth and Form: The complete revised edition*, p.16, Dover Publications, Inc., New York, 1992 (first published by Cambridge University Press as *On Growth and Form: A New Edition*, 1942, written in 1917).

44   Ibid., p.57

45   Ibid., p.289

46   Le Corbusier, op. cit., p.153

47   Gregory, 1997, op. cit., p.180

48   World Commission on Environment and Development, *Our Common Future*, 1987, Oxford University Press, reprinted 2009.

49   Data extracted from the US Energy Information Administration 2012 Commercial Buildings Energy Consumption Survey (CBECS), revised April 2015, available from: http://www.eia.gov/consumption/commercial/data/2012/#b2

50   http://energy.gov/sites/prod/files/maprod/documents/HPSB-MOU.pdf

51   Ibid.

52   United States General Service Administration website: http://www.gsa.gov/portal/content/104462

53   Ibid.

54   *Expanding Our Approach to Sustainable Design – An Invitation*, U.S. General Services Administration, submitted by BuildingGreen, Inc. 12/15/2005.

55   Ibid., pp.9 and 13

56   Ibid., p.19

57   Ibid., p.9

58   Ibid., p.13

59   Morphopedia website, Morphosis: http://morphopedia.com/projects/bill-melinda-gates-hall (accessed 31 December 2014)

60   *Morphosis Computes a Facade for Cornell*, A|N Blog, Architecture Newspaper, available from: http://blog.archpaper.com/2014/12/morphosis-computes-facade-cornell/ (accessed December 2014).
     "'The goal was to establish a consistent level of daylighting throughout the interior,' said Cory Brugger, director of design technology at Morphosis. 'We maximized the exterior glazing to get the light coming through. The design of the screen reduces the amount of glare and heat gain and starts to help with the performance of the facade system itself.'"

61   A. Zahner Co. website, manufacturer of the solar shade panels for Gates Hall, http://www.azahner.com/portfolio/gates-hall-cornell, December 31, 2014

62   Morhopedia website, Morphosis, http://morphopedia.com/projects/bill-melinda-gates-hall, December 31, 2014

63   National Architectural Accrediting Board, Inc., *2009 Conditions for Accreditation*, p.4, Washington, DC, approved 10 July 2009.

64   www.naab.org/about/home and paraphrased at www.ncarb.org/Studying-Architecture/Overview-Of-Architectural-Education.aspx (accessed 4 March 2014)

65   *Student Performance Criteria* (SPC), DRAFT #3 'Comments & References' – SPC plus Conditions Task Group 02.14.08, National Architectural Accrediting Board

(NAAB), GENERAL COMMENTS of the Evolving Conditions and SPC Task Group 2/14/08.

66   Architectural Education & Accreditation, *ACSA Report for the Accreditation Review Conference, Assessment of the 2009 Conditions*, Association of Collegiate Schools of Architecture, Washington, DC, available from: http://www.acsa-arch.org/docs/resources/acsa-arc-position-paper.pdf?sfvrsn=2.

67   *NAAB Conditions for Accreditation For Professional Degree Programs in Architecture*, 2004 Edition; *2009 Conditions for Accreditation*, approved 10 July 2009; *2014 Conditions for Accreditation National Architectural Accrediting Board*, Inc, approved 18 July 2014, National Architectural Accrediting Board, Inc., Washington, DC.

68   AIA CONTINUING EDUCATION SYSTEM, *AIA Board Mainstreams Sustainable Design Education*, 2015, available from: http://www.aia.org/education/ces/AIAS076973 (accessed 12 January 2015).

69   Gilles Deleuze, *The Fold: Leibniz and the Baroque*, Chapters 1 and 2, translated by Tom Conley, University of Minnesota Press, 1993, originally published as *Le Pli: Leibniz et le baroque*, Les Editions de Minuit, Paris, 1988.

70   Robert Venturi, *Complexity and Contradiction in Architecture*, pp.74–8, Museum of Modern Art, New York, Second edition 1977, reprinted 2002.

71   Ibid., p.86

72   Luca Finocchiaro and Anne Grete Hestnes, Symbiosis and Mimesis in the Built Environment, *Aesthetics of Sustainable Archietcture*, p.261, edited by Sang Lee, 010 Publishers, Rotterdam, 2011.

73   Ibid., pp.260–1

74   Ibid., p.260

75   Deleuze, op. cit., p.14

76   Peter Macapia, *Singularity, Peter Macapia studio*, Pratt Institute Graduate School of Architecture and Urban Design, Spring 2009.

77   Peter Macapia, email exchange with author, 15–19 June 2012.

78   Deleuze, op. cit., p.15

79   Peter Macapia, email exchange with author, 15–19 June 2012.

80   Deleuze, op. cit., p.14

81   James J. Gibson, *The Ecological Approach to Visual Perception*, pp.16–19, Psychology Press, Taylor & Francis Group, New York, 1986.

82   Ibid., p.16

83   Ibid., p.39

84   Ibid., p.23, emphasis added by author

85   Leonardo Da Vinci selected by Irma A. Ricter, edited by Thereza Wells, *Notebooks / Leonardo Da Vinci*, p.120, Oxford University Press, New York, 1952, 2008.

86   Avrum Stroll, *Surfaces*, University of Minnesota Press, Minneapolis, MN, 1988.

87   Ibid., p.208

88   Ibid., p.45

89   Ibid., pp.49–50

90   Gibson, op. cit., pp.16, 39 and 127

91   Sang Lee and Stefanie Holzheu, 'Building Envelope as Surface', *Aesthetics for Sustainable Architecture*, Sang Lee, editor, p.128, 010 Publishers, Rotterdam, 2011.

92 Ibid., pp.128–9

93 Ibid., p.128

94 Gottfried Semper, *Style in the Technical and Tectonic Arts; or, Practical Aesthetics*, (Der Stil in den technischen und tektonischen Kunsten; oder, Praktische Aesthetik: Ein Handbuch fur Techniker), pp.153–4, Kunstler und Kunstfreunde, 2 vols (Frankfurt am Main: Verlag fur Kunst & Wissenschaft. 1860: Munich: F. Bruckmann, 1863), Translation by Harry Francis Mallgrave & Michael Robinson, Getty Research Institute, Los Angeles, 2004.

95 Vitruvius, op. cit., pp.15–16

96 Halprin, op. cit.

97 Ibid., p.141

98 Ibid., pp.135, 138–9; sketch provided by the Architectural Archives, University of Pennsylvania by the gift of Lawrence Halprin.

99 Ibid.; sketch provided by the Architectural Archives, University of Pennsylvania by the gift of Lawrence Halprin.

100 Vitruvius, op. cit., p.24

101 Eero Saarinen, *Eero Saarinen on his Work*, p.60, edited by Aline B. Saarinen, Yale University Press, 1962.

102 Ibid., p.6

103 Ibid., pp.6 and 14

104 http://www.orrefors.us/products/street-decanter-6540183

105 Ada Louise Huxtable, 'Found – and Lost – in Translation', *Wall Street Journal*, 6 February 2008, available from: http://online.wsj.com/news/articles/ SB120226053029946053
"This is helicopter architecture, dropped down anywhere, delivering extreme, iconic images totally detached from place or past, dedicated to billion-dollar deals and million-dollar condos. Its purpose is to knock your socks off."

106 Edith Wharton and Ogden Codman, *The Decoration of Houses*, p. xix, Charles Scribner's Sons, 1897, facsimile printing by HardPress Publishing, Miami, Florida.

107 Ibid., p.64

108 Ibid., pp.65–7

109 As in the case of photocatalytic paints containing titanium dioxide.

110 Karim Elgendy, *Energy Efficient Design in the Middle East: Approaches and Challenges*, SatchNet Electronic Systems, 23 October 2010, based on *Approaches and challenges to energy efficiency in the Middle East,* BuildGreen, Dubai, October 2010.

111 Mohammad Al-Asad and Tareq Emtairah, 'Cities and Buildings', *Arab Environment 4: Green Economy, Sustainable Transition in a Changing Arab World*, 2011 Report of the Arab Forum for Environment and Development, pp.180–1, published with *Technical Publications and Environment & Development* magazine, Beirut, Lebanon.

112 Wael Al-Masri, Chief Architect, Wael Al-Masri Planners & Architects, 'Environmental Sustainability in Traditional Arab Architecture', *Arab Environment 4: Green Economy, Sustainable Transition in a Changing Arab World*, 2011 Report of the Arab Forum for Environment and Development, pp.198–9, published with *Technical Publications and Environment & Development* magazine, Beirut, Lebanon.

Wael Al-Masri is the Chief Architect at Wael Al-Masri Planners & Architects in Amman, Jordan.

113 Ibid.

114 Alvaro Viegas, *Role of Architectural Super Graphics in Generating Identities in Urban Environments (Focusing on the Narrative Patterns of Super Graphics)*, p.4, National Institute of Design, India, April 2011, available from: http://issuu.com/alva-roviegas/docs/identityandsupergraphics (accessed 1 April 2014).

115 Doug Aitken, *SONG 1*, projected on the exterior of the Hirshhorn Museum in Washington DC in 2012.

116 Doug Aitken, *Lighthouse*, projected on the exterior of the Art Barn, Hudson Valley, NY in 2012.

117 Sylvia Lavin, *Kissing Architecture*, Princeton University Press, Princeton, NJ, 2011.

118 Details of the Stradella Road residence were provided by Randy Reiss during the author's visit in August 2015 and in subsequent email exchanges in September 2015; and by a phone interview with the designer of the Stradella Road residence, architect David Hertz FAIA, on 2 September 2015 and in subsequent email exchanges. Additional information was obtained from *The Lehrer Residence: A Case Study in Resource Efficient Alternates*, and *The Natural House*, Nick Madigan, The Outlook, Santa Monica, CA, 5 October 1996.

119 Madigan, op. cit.

120 All photographs of the Stradella Road residence were taken by the author with the generous permission of Randy Reiss.

121 Email exchange and phone interview of David Hertz FAIA, designer of the Stradella Road House on 2 September 2015 and Randy Reiss.

122 *2011 Buildings Energy Data Book*, U.S. Department of Energy, Building Technologies Program, Energy Efficiency and Renewable Energy, by D&R International, Ltd, March 2012.

123 *Building and Climate Change: Summary for Decision-Makers*, Sustainable Buildings & Climate Initiative, UNEP DTIE, Sustainable Consumption & Production Branch, Paris, France, United Nations Environment Programme, 2009.

124 Ibid., p.2

125 Ibid., p.14

126 *2011 Buildings Energy Data Book*, op. cit., Table 1.6.1

127 *2011 Buildings Energy Data Book*, op. cit., Table 5.2.8

128 Lance Hosey, *The Shape of Green: Aesthetics, Ecology, and Design*, Epilogue, p.179, Island Press, Washington, DC, 2012.